The UN General Assembly

The UN General Assembly is arguably the most important forum for the discussion of global politics. This guide traces how it has both reflected and accentuated the changing dynamics of global politics by providing an environment for global deliberations, an arena for conflict, and an additional site for diplomacy and transnational issue advocacy.

The book addresses:

- development of the General Assembly
- the General Assembly process
- the General Assembly in relation to the member states and the rest of the UN system
- criticisms of the General Assembly
- the assembly in the twenty-first century.

The UN General Assembly provides a balanced view of this institution, assessing its role and future whilst also addressing the various criticisms of the assembly. This is an ideal book for students of the United Nations, international organizations, and global governance.

M.J. Peterson is Professor of Political Science at the University of Massachusetts Amherst, where she teaches courses on world politics, international organizations, and international law. She is the author of *The General Assembly in World Politics* (London, 1986), a study of the General Assembly's institutional development during its first 40 years of existence.

Global Institutions Series

Edited by Thomas G. Weiss

The CUNY Graduate Center, New York, USA

and Rorden Wilkinson

University of Manchester, UK

About the series

The "Global Institutions Series" is edited by Thomas G. Weiss (the CUNY Graduate Center, New York, USA) and Rorden Wilkinson (University of Manchester, UK), and designed to provide readers with comprehensive, accessible, and informative guides to the history, structure, and activities of key international organizations. Every volume stands on its own as a thorough and insightful treatment of a particular topic, but the series as a whole contributes to a coherent and complementary portrait of the phenomenon of global institutions at the dawn of the millennium.

Each book is written by a recognized expert in the field, conforms to a similar structure, and covers a range of themes and debates common to the series. These areas of shared concern include the general purpose and rationale for organizations, developments over time, membership, structure, decision-making procedures, and key functions. Moreover, the current debates are placed in a historical perspective alongside informed analysis and critique. Each book also contains an annotated bibliography and guide to electronic information as well as any annexes appropriate to the subject matter at hand. The volumes currently under contract include:

The United Nations and Human Rights (2005)
A Guide for a New Era
by Julie Mertus (American University)

UN Global Conferences (2005)
by Michael Schechter (Michigan State University)

The UN Secretary-General and Secretariat (2005)
by Leon Gordenker (Princeton University)

The UN General Assembly (2005)
by M.J. Peterson (University of Massachusetts, Amherst)

Group of 7/8
by Hugo Dobson (University of Sheffield)

The World Bank
From Reconstruction to Development to Equity
by Katherine Marshall (World Bank)

The International Organization
for Standardization and the
Global Economy
Setting Standards
*by Craig Murphy (Wellesley College)
and JoAnne Yates (Massachusetts
Institute of Technology)*

The World Trade Organization
*by Bernard Hoekman (World Bank) and
Petros Mavroidis (Columbia University)*

For further information regarding the series, please contact:

Craig Fowlie, Publisher, Politics & International Studies
Taylor & Francis
2 Park Square, Milton Park, Abingdon
Oxford OX14 4RN, UK

+44 (0)207 842 2057 Tel
+44 (0)207 842 2302 Fax

Craig.Fowlie@tandf.co.uk
www.routledge.com

The UN General Assembly

M.J. Peterson

Routledge
Taylor & Francis Group

LONDON AND NEW YORK

First published 2006
by Routledge
2 Park Square, Milton Park, Abingdon, Oxon OX14 4RN

Simultaneously published in the USA and Canada
by Routledge
270 Madison Ave, New York, NY 10016

Routledge is an imprint of the Taylor & Francis Group

© 2006 M.J. Peterson

Typeset in Garamond by
Taylor & Francis Books
Printed and bound in Great Britain by
TJ International Ltd, Padstow, Cornwall

British Library Cataloguing in Publication Data
A catalogue record for this book is available
from the British Library

Library of Congress Cataloging in Publication Data
A catalog record for this book has been requested

ISBN10 0– 415–34388–7 (hbk)
ISBN10 0– 415–34389–5 (pbk)

ISBN13 9–78–0–415–34388–7 (hbk)
ISBN13 9–78-0–415–34389–5 (pbk)

T&F informa

Taylor & Francis Group is the Academic Division of T&F Informa plc.

Contents

Foreword

The current volume is the fourth in a new and dynamic series on "Global Institutions." This one offers a comprehensive guide to the history, structure, and concrete activities of one of the world organization's six principal organs, "the UN General Assembly." Remarkable as it may seem, there exist relatively few books that offer in-depth treatments of prominent global bodies and processes, much less an entire series of concise and complementary volumes. Those that do exist are either out of date, inaccessible to the non-specialist reader, or seek to develop a specialized understanding of particular aspects of an institution or a process rather than offer an overall account of its functioning. Similarly, existing books have often been written in highly technical language or have been crafted "in-house" and are notoriously self-serving and narrow in focus.

The advent of electronic media has helped by making public information and resolutions more widely available, but it has also complicated matters further. The growing reliance on the internet and other electronic methods of finding information about key international organizations and processes have served, ironically, to limit the educational materials to which most readers have ready access – namely, books. Public relations documents, raw data, and loosely refereed websites do not intelligent analysis make. Official publications compete with a vast amount of electronically available information, much of which is suspect because of its ideological or self-promoting slant. Paradoxically, the growing range of purportedly independent websites offering analyses of the activities of particular organizations have emerged, but one inadvertent consequence has been to frustrate access to basic, authoritative, critical, and well-researched texts. The market for such has actually been reduced by the ready availability of varying-quality electronic materials.

We are delighted that Routledge asked us to edit a series that bucks this trend. They are betting that serious students and professionals will want serious analyses. We have assembled a first-rate line-up of authors to address that market. Our intention, then, is to provide one-stop shopping for all readers – students (both undergraduate and postgraduate), interested negotiators, diplomats, practitioners from nongovernmental and intergovernmental organizations, and interested parties alike – seeking information about the most prominent institutional aspects of global governance.

The UN General Assembly

We asked M.J. Peterson – Professor of Political Science at the University of Massachusetts Amherst – to undertake the daunting task of making sense of what many see as the globe's parliament, or at least the closest thing that we have to one at the moment. We could not have found a commentator with more analytical experience who could write more clearly about this complex topic. A leading scholar of international relations and long-time editor of the journal *Polity*, she wrote one the first and still most widely cited books about this topic, *The General Assembly in World Politics*.[1] And much of her distinguished career as a teacher and researcher has focused on the behavior and misbehavior of the United Nations, including her recent investigation of the General Assembly's role in dealing with the blight of terrorism.[2]

M.J. Peterson's concise yet comprehensive volume will permit readers to understand the strengths and weaknesses of the arena in which 191 member states of the United Nations debate issues of global import. There are two extremes of criticism often voiced about the General Assembly. On the one hand, it is dismissed as a tunnel of "hot air" or "paper mill" of useless resolutions. On the other hand, and based largely on his exposure to the General Assembly, the late US Senator Daniel Patrick Moynihan put forward a different view: he called his memoir about his eight months as United States Permanent Representative to the United Nations in 1975 and 1976 "a dangerous place."[3]

Which is it? Clearly, the stage on which presidents and prime ministers, diplomats and international civil servants pronounce themselves about the nature of global problems and their solutions is a highly "politicized" one in which the so-called success or failure of initiatives, like beauty, lies in the eyes of the beholder. For Peterson, complaining that the General Assembly is politicized is really beside the point: "Such complaint is reasonable when raised against a body that is supposed to make decisions based on some other logic – for instance the legal reasoning used by a court or the expert reasoning used by a technical commission. However, the General Assembly is a political body, and participants have never pretended otherwise."

Our hope is that M.J. Peterson's analysis reaches a broad audience with its many useful descriptions, lists of resources, and numerous concrete examples that illustrate the essential role of the General Assembly in world politics. As always, we welcome comments and suggestions from readers.

Thomas G. Weiss, the CUNY Graduate Center, New York, USA
Rorden Wilkinson, University of Manchester, UK
February 2005

Notes

1 M.J. Peterson, *The General Assembly in World Politics* (Boston: Unwin Hyman, 1986).
2 M.J. Peterson, "Using the General Assembly," in Jane Boulden and Thomas G. Weiss (eds), *Terrorism and the UN: Before and after September 11* (Bloomington: Indiana University Press, 2004), pp.173–97.
3 Daniel Patrick Moynihan, *A Dangerous Place* (Boston: Little, Brown & Co., 1978).

Preface

Rational choice theorists derive considerable analytical traction from the "shadow of the future," but life is also affected by the "shadow of the past." This book is one example of an academic shadow of the past, a request to revisit a subject researched earlier, update previous knowledge, and present the results to peers or wider readerships. An invitation by Tom Weiss and Rorden Wilkinson to contribute to their series on "Global Institutions" triggered this return to a topic that I initially explored about 20 years ago.

Though the context in which the UN General Assembly operates has been changed considerably by the events of those 20 years, the institution itself displays strong continuities. The same problems of accommodating a large membership and a long agenda remain central to its internal functioning. The same problem of living in the shadows − of superpower competition, G-7 summits, and UN global conferences in the 1980s; of G-7 summits, global conferences, and a revived Security Council today − inhibits developing a coherent institutional role for it.

The General Assembly, like other political institutions, is shaped by its founders, influences its current members' behavior, and is reshaped by their conduct. They are thus human creations that take on the characteristics of a "social fact" existing as individual reality outside the will of each member, but amenable to modification as the wider political context changes or as intentional and unintentional consequences of its members' choices and interactions accumulate. The end of the Cold War freed the whole UN system, including the General Assembly, from the constraints of East−West ideological competition and looming danger of the third world war under which it had operated since the late 1940s. Yet the anticipated blossoming of international co-operation and renewal of the UN system has not occurred because the members have not developed enough of a shared sense of what they want the UN system to be. This problem is particularly acute in the General Assembly, where institutional inertia is particularly strong because it serves various members' purposes.

Never having held an official position in the UN or any government, I do not have to repeat here the standard disclaimer that the views expressed are those of the author and not of any organization, government, or agency. I am happy to acknowledge that this book is much better than the first draft because of helpful comments from Thomas G. Weiss, Rorden Wilkinson, Effie Maclachlan, and Ausama Abdelhadi. Ms Maclachlan also took computer files full of oddities produced by Microsoft Word's baffling default settings and made a coherent manuscript of it. Craig Fowlie and his crew at Routledge took it through the production process with stunning efficiency.

1 Overview

Characteristics of the General Assembly

Article 7 of the Charter establishes the General Assembly as one of six "principal organs" of the United Nations (UN). It is the only one of the six that includes representatives of all member states, simultaneously respecting and confirming their sovereign equality by giving each of them one vote, regardless of military power, wealth, population, size of territory, or any other characteristic. Historically, it is successor to the Assembly of the League of Nations. The League Assembly also included representatives of all member states but tended to be overshadowed by the League Council, where the foreign ministers of the major powers often met to address the major crises of the day. As decolonization brought former colonies into the organization, the UN General Assembly has evolved from a fifty-one-member body drawn, like its League predecessor, mainly from Europe and Latin America to a 191-member body with a primarily African and Asian membership. More constant, and also building on League experience, has been the use of regional and other caucusing groups to organize the members into clusters that give structure to interactions (see Chapter 3).

Its egalitarian treatment of member states and worldwide composition make the General Assembly the pre-eminent global deliberative body. Some hope and others fear that it is the germ of a true global legislature. In their Millennium Declaration, the member states reaffirmed its place as "the chief deliberative, policy-making, and representative organ of the United Nations."[1] Yet its deliberations are currently overshadowed by the Security Council and global summits. Its own inability to break from a mind-numbing routine of adopting a resolution on nearly all of the more than 150 items on its agenda each year deepens its obscurity and confirms its modest hold on media and public attention.

Primary functions

Article 10 of the UN Charter gives the General Assembly two primary functions. It authorizes the assembly to "discuss any questions or any matters within the scope of the present Charter ... and, except as provided in article 12 ... make recommendations to the Members of the United Nations or to the Security Council or to both on any such questions or matters." This is the basis of the assembly's claim to be the pre-eminent global deliberative body. It also authorizes the assembly to discuss and make recommendations regarding "the powers and functions of any organs provided for in the present Charter." Article 10 is thus the basis of the assembly's place as the center of the whole UN system (even though the Charter lists it as one of six "principal organs"), authorizes creation of additional subsidiary organs, and establishes a network of functionally differentiated specialized agencies.

Deliberative body

Even with its original membership of 51 states, sending several hundred delegates, the General Assembly was far too large to be an executive council. Nor could it serve as an administrative agency because its sessions were initially limited to the fall season. Executive functions were allocated elsewhere, to the Security Council, the Economic and Social Council, and the Trusteeship Council, while administrative functions were given to the Secretariat and the task of promoting co-operation in particular administrative or technical areas to the specialized agencies.

Like its interwar predecessor, the General Assembly drew on a combination of Western diplomatic and parliamentary practice in developing its methods of work. The one state–one vote rule, and rules regarding such matters as seating of delegations in the meeting rooms, drew on the practices of international conferences as developed in Europe and the Americas. The rules governing formal debate in public meetings drew partly on international practice, and partly on practices used in European national legislatures. These rules, with their emphasis on formal proposals, public discussion, and offering of amendments or alternate proposals at public meetings, were more or less familiar to different delegations. They were very familiar to delegates from the Americas, the British "Old Dominions" of Australia, Canada, New Zealand, and South Africa, and other former British colonies like India and Pakistan since all had national legislatures on the European model. They were less familiar in the cultures of the Middle East, Africa, and Asia – despite several decades of European colonialism or other domination – though many of the leaders of these countries were educated in the West or acquainted with the rules through their understanding of interwar diplomacy.

All delegations have been keenly aware of the strong tension between the one state–one vote rule prevailing inside the assembly and the traditional practices of power politics diplomacy and bilateral bargaining outside. The playing out of this tension has been one of the enduring themes in the General Assembly's evolution. It became increasingly prominent as the US-led majority of the late 1940s and early 1950s, was replaced in the late 1950s by a set of fluid alignments and in the early 1960s by a Third World majority anchored initially in an Afro-Asian bloc and then in the Nonaligned Movement and the Group of 77. The assembly's increasing resort to making decisions by consensus rather than voting is one way to resolve the tension, and has also been encouraged by its appeal to delegates from non-Western areas where various forms of consensus-building are – or are claimed to be – more consistent with their culture.

As UN membership expanded, and the number of items on its agenda increased, the assembly was increasingly hard pressed to complete its work within the approximately 13 weeks of the regular annual session following its formal rules of procedure. It responded in two ways. It expanded the time available by resuming sessions in the spring or holding special sessions on particular topics generally perceived as particularly important. It also speeded deliberations on particular items through a set of unwritten practices for circulating drafts, presenting amendments or rival proposals, and developing a single draft through informal consultations held outside the public meetings. When deliberation in the assembly is on track to produce consensus, delegates shift to these informal practices, and formal proceedings are reduced to a minimum. However, the formal rules of procedure remain in effect, and can be invoked whenever any delegation so wishes.

Seeing the General Assembly as a proto-world parliament is encouraged by its status as the only principal UN organ including all member states and the similarity between its formal rules of procedure and the rules of parliamentary practice used in national legislatures. This vision is particularly strong among World Federalists and others who believe that establishing a world government is necessary to securing a more just and orderly international system. It has been expressed in more immediate terms by those international lawyers who argue that the General Assembly has already acquired authority to make international law, that is, to adopt rules binding on UN member states.

Many international reformers and international lawyers are guided by the domestic analogy, the notion that an orderly political system must be centralized, with political institutions making and applying common rules to every state and person around the world. In this discourse, the "anarchy" of the states system is contrasted with the "order" prevailing within states. Replicating at the global level the sorts of central legislative, administrative, and police institutions found in states is seen as the solution to the problems of avoiding war, improving the distribution of material well-being, ensuring respect for human rights, and maintaining ecological sustainability.

The notion that lack of world government leaves the world in an anarchy resembling a Hobbesian state of nature, in which states struggle constantly for power and existence, acquired strong plausibility from the hard-edged pursuit of power politics that characterized much of the twentieth century and is far from over today. However, it is possible to conceive of world order based on decentralized modes of governance, whether through closer co-operation among states or through transnational networks (see Chapter 6). Proponents acknowledge that these are effective only when the various members of the world community (whether states, groups, or individuals) understand that they have common or parallel interests and are interdependent on each other's choices and efforts. For these observers, forums like the General Assembly serve as places for developing and reaffirming the sense of commonality and interdependence rather than as proto-legislatures.

Ambitious global reformers, inspired by the domestic analogy, criticize these more decentralized visions because they entail maintaining the current process of developing obligatory international principles, norms, and rules through the relatively slow processes of developing customary international law or negotiating and winning ratification of multilateral treaties. Many global reformers argue that the increasing pace of technological, social, and cultural change requires moving away from those older processes. Yet in their anxiety, they mistake the end-phase of the national law-making process – when a proposal is finally debated and voted upon in the national legislature – for the whole. Even within countries, ideas disseminate slowly, policy initiatives meet with various forms of active and passive resistance, and proposals that in retrospect seem so obviously right that they should have sailed through the process, get defeated when first presented.

Governments remain very clear about where they stand in this debate. They have not transferred legislative authority to the General Assembly. This was stated directly on three occasions during the 1970s, and there has been no significant modification of the position since. In a 1973 discussion of the International Court of Justice's role in resolving disputes between states, delegates from the Congo, Ivory Coast, Kenya, Kuwait, and Mexico proposed stating that, "the International Court of Justice should take into account those developments in international law reflected in declarations and resolutions adopted by the United Nations General Assembly."[2] Other delegates objected, and the formulation actually adopted read: "recognizing that the development of international law may be reflected, inter alia, by declarations and resolutions of the General Assembly which may to that extent be taken into consideration by the International Court of Justice."[3] Some Third World legal specialists suggested that their governments should condemn the unilateral deep-seabed mining legislation adopted by the USA in 1979 as illegal under international law because it violated the "common heritage of mankind" principle established in the General Assembly's Declaration of Principles governing the Seabed.[4] However, governments had foreseen such arguments and made clear in 1970 that they did not regard that Declaration as creating a legal rule. Most critics of US and other states' moves toward unilateral or small-group seabed mining arrangements were careful to base their arguments on the Law of the Sea Convention itself. Even delegates on the vehemently anti-Israel Committee on the Exercise of the Inalienable Rights of the Palestinian People backed off from endorsing conclusions that Israel had violated international law when acting contrary to General Assembly resolutions in 1979.[5] The committee has relied far more on insisting that the Geneva Conventions on the conduct of war apply and that Israel is violating the rules regarding treatment of occupied territories and populations. Thus most international lawyers have been circumspect in their claims regarding General Assembly authority. Richard Falk referred to a "quasi-legislative" role[6] while others emphasized that any such role was limited to certain occasions,[7] and yet others frankly admitted that they were advocating a proposal rather than describing a reality.[8]

Concluding that the General Assembly does not directly create international law rules binding on member states does not mean that it is irrelevant to the development of globally shared norms and rules. It constantly engages in norm-creation and norm-adjustment as it accepts new issues onto the international agenda, considers new ideas, debates the relative merits of competing positions, and attempts to formulate statements of goals and methods for achieving them that will win widespread support. Many of the ideas first expressed in assembly resolutions have been incorporated in multilateral treaties or adopted into state practice enough to become customary international law.

Definer of the UN system

The United Nations was a sprawling system of related bodies and agencies even in 1945. Sprawl has increased over the years as new committees, commissions, expert groups, programs, and agencies were established and hardly any terminated. The Security Council, the Economic and Social Council, and the Trusteeship Council have authority under the Charter to create subsidiary bodies of their own and the specialized agencies are also masters of their own structure. However, the Charter gives the General Assembly the widest authority to define the structure of the UN system. It cannot alter the features – such as the existence of six "principal organs" and of the specialized agencies, the membership, voting rules, and functions of those principal organs, and procedures for admitting or expelling member states – defined in the Charter itself. Only the member states, using the amendment procedure defined in Articles 108 and 109, can do that. However, the assembly can reorganize much of the UN structure through its authority over the budget, its ability to reorganize the Secretariat, and its power to create its own subsidiary bodies.

Such decisions have implications for member states because they create or restructure organizational activity. Governments largely accept that the assembly can create what Ingrid Detter called "external administrative rules" regulating the relations between the UN and themselves.[9] These specify how to comply with provisions of the Charter or accomplish various routine organizational tasks, and stem directly from the fact of being a member. On occasion, they resist and seek to withhold the portion of their assessment going to some program or activity they particularly dislike, but even the US government, the most frequent practitioner of this form of protest, singles out a relatively small number of UN programs for this treatment. More often, they co-operate to limit the implications of assembly decisions by specifying that they will be supported by voluntary contributions rather than the regular UN budget (Chapter 4 discusses the politics of the budget in more detail).

A few international lawyers have claimed that the General Assembly acquires some additional authority when, substituting for a deadlocked Security Council, it invokes the "Uniting for Peace" resolution procedures for dealing with crises at an emergency session. Though the Uniting for Peace resolution was highly controversial when first adopted (see Chapter 4) advocates of this view claim that later use of the "Uniting for Peace" procedure by the original opponents means all UN member governments have accepted it as consistent with the Charter.[10] They acknowledge that the assembly cannot order collective measures under Chapter VII of the Charter. However, advocates maintain that assembly resolutions recommending collective measures do release member states from their normal obligations to avoid threat or use of armed force against the target state and from any treaty obligations they may have towards it regarding nondiscrimination in trade, investment, and other sorts of transactions.[11] The assembly can create or continue a UN peacekeeping operation or a truce observation mission, but these – like their Security Council-created counterparts – have involved only those states willing to contribute troops, and remain in place only as long as a government desires their presence on its territory.

Articles 73 and 74 of the Charter give the assembly key roles in decolonization. Article 73 gives the assembly authority to determine what territories are non-self-governing, and therefore administered by UN member states under the principles established in Articles 73 and 74. Some metropole governments did ignore its declarations, the longest running being Portuguese refusal to submit reports on its colonial territories between 1956 (when it was admitted to membership) and 1974 (when a military coup overthrew the right-wing dictatorship). Most, however, acknowledged its authority and sought to avoid certain listings rather than challenge the principle that the assembly can make them. Article 74 established the assembly as ultimate supervisor of Trust Territories, and gave it the authority to end Trusteeship arrangements.[12]

Some of the General Assembly's difficulties over the years have stemmed from the fact the UN system has seldom worked as anticipated. In the original design, dealing with crisis situations that were likely to worsen into war was left to the Security Council, detailed supervision of colonial administration to the Trusteeship Council, and detailed coordination of UN system activities on economic and social concerns to the Economic and Social Council. The Security Council was largely deadlocked between 1947 and 1986, only functioning as anticipated when the ideologically divided "Permanent 5" agreed to use it. The Trusteeship Council never supervised as many colonial administrations as hoped because most colonies were kept outside the Trusteeship System, and lost all role in 1994 when the last of the eleven Trust Territories became independent. The Economic and Social Council failed to develop as planned for reasons to be explored in Chapter 4.

Security Council deadlock meant that for many years the General Assembly was more prominent within the UN system than anticipated in the Charter. However this did not translate into greater prominence in the international system. The UN as a whole failed to function as planned because the governments of the world did not share the degree of normative or pragmatic consensus required to the UN as designed. The obstacles became less formidable with the end of the Cold War, but in the eyes of the world the General Assembly was overshadowed by a newly active Security Council and a series of global conferences and summits.

Plan of the book

Both the General Assembly and its relation to other global institutions inside and outside the United Nations have evolved considerably in the 60 years since 1945. Chapter 2 will examine the highlights of the historical development of the assembly, beginning with the expectations of 1945, their disappointment during the Cold War, the new directions taken as decolonization led to vast expansion of the UN membership, and continued change since the end of the Cold War. With the main features of the changing political context laid out, Chapter 3 will examine the process by which the assembly accomplishes its work. After identifying the various types of actors involved, it will focus on both the formal rules of procedure and informal practices regulating the formulation and adoption of resolutions and other decisions. Chapter 4 will focus outward, assessing assembly interactions with the UN member states and other elements of the UN system. Chapter 5 will examine the basis and weight of several criticisms of the assembly that have been made in one form or another since 1945. Chapter 6 will look forward, examining how three possible futures of the international system – a continued world of states, a shift to world government, or development of a world of networks – will affect how the assembly develops.

Notes

1 General Assembly Resolution 55/2 of 8 September 2000, Section VIII. Accessible through *www.un.org/general assembly/resolutions*.
2 A/29/Annex 93, 2.
3 Resolution 3232 (XXIX) eighth preambular paragraph, in A/29/Annex 93, p. 2.
4 GA Resolution 2749 (XXV) of 1970.
5 See prefatory note stating that neither the Special Committee itself nor the UN Secretariat necessarily endorsed that view, UN Doc. ST/SG/SER.F/4 September 1979.
6 Richard A. Falk, "On the quasi-legislative competence of the General Assembly," *American Journal of International Law* 60: 782–91 (1966).
7 Rosalyn Higgins, The Development of International Law through the Political Organs of the United Nations (Oxford: 1963); M.N. Shaw, Title to Territory in Africa (Oxford: 1986).
8 For example Oscar Schachter, "The relation of law, politics, and action in the United Nations," Hague Academy of International Law *Recueil des cours* 109: 184–6 (1963); Samuel A. Bleicher, "The legal significance of re-citation of General Assembly resolutions," *American Journal of International Law* 63: 447 (1963); Taslim O. Elias, *Africa and the Development of International Law* (Leiden: 1972), 71–6; Louis B. Sohn, "The development of the United Nations Charter," in Maarten Bos (ed.) *The Present State of International Law* (Deventer: 1973), 50–3.
9 Ingrid Detter, *Law Making by International Organizations* (Stockholm: 1965), chapter 1, sections 4–5; also the International Court of Justice Advisory Opinion on Certain Expenses of the United Nations, *ICJ Reports 1962*, 162–3.
10 See Jorge Casteñeda, *The Legal Effects of United Nations Resolutions* (New York: 1969), 81–107.
11 E.g. Casteñeda, *Legal Effects,* 107–16; Christoph Schreuer, "Recommendations and the traditional sources of international law," *German Yearbook of International Law* 20: 118 (1977).
12 See International Court of Justice ruling in the Case concerning the Northern Cameroons, *ICJ Reports 1963*, 32 and Advisory Opinion on Namibia (South West Africa), *ICJ Reports 1971*, 50.

2 Development of the General Assembly

Political institutions are sites of interaction that develop and change over time in reaction to shifts in the broader social context and in actors' beliefs, expectations, and behavior. Both social context – the global distribution of political power and economic activity – and actor beliefs, expectations, and behavior have shifted considerably in the six decades since 1945. Though the basic characteristics of the General Assembly have remained the same, its impact on world politics and the extent to which it was or was not viewed as a precursor to a global legislature have altered considerably. While some chroniclers see a pattern of constant decline from the high expectations of the late 1940s,[1] the story is a bit more complicated. However, it is clear that without significant changes in its ways, the General Assembly will become irrelevant.

Expectations in 1945

The main features of the United Nations had been determined before the Germans surrendered in May 1945 and the Japanese in August. Already foreseeing victory, the "Big 3" and other Allies agreed in late 1943 that they needed to create a new general international organization to maintain the postwar international order and deal with the new problems that were likely to arise. As foreseen in the Teheran Declaration of 1 December 1943 and the Dumbarton Oaks proposals of October 1944, the UN Charter established a clearer division of labor between the Security Council and the General Assembly than had prevailed between the League of Nations Council and Assembly. In the Security Council, the great powers would take the lead in managing a revised collective security system. In the General Assembly, the entire membership would deliberate on and identify solutions to the various political, military, economic, and social problems of the day. A host of affiliated agencies would promote co-operation on particular administrative and technical matters through promoting joint discussion and parallel action among the ministry or government agency in each member state handling that matter. Based on elements of earlier experience elaborated in the Functionalist theory of David Mitrany,[2] this part of the plan brought the older public international unions, the new international technical agencies created during the war, and any that might be established later into the United Nations as Specialized Agencies.

As representatives of the victorious governments assembled in San Francisco in April 1945, they brought great hopes, but not the same fervent expectation of imminent transformation in international relations that had inspired advocates of the League of Nations in 1919. Use of atomic bombs against Japan had demonstrated a new technological possibility that reinforced the already strong consensus on the need to avert a third world war. However, there was greater appreciation than in 1919 that political unrest and hard-edged power politics were likely to persist, and could become as brutal as they had been in the 1930s unless governments co-operated with each other better. All the while, governments based their planning, and publics their visions of the near future, on certain expectations about the postwar world that shaped their initial attitudes towards the United Nations. They expected that the co-operation forged among members of the anti-Axis coalition would continue after the war. The great powers would act in concert to avoid another world war, Functionalist co-operation would lead to improved economic and social conditions, and thereby reduce the roots of conflict, and the international system would be transformed from a Europe-centered to a global one through a gradual process of decolonization.

Continuation of the Anti-Fascist Coalition

The San Francisco Conference was a gathering of the victors; delegates from Germany, Italy, and Japan, and any state that had not declared war on the Axis before 1 March 1944 were not invited. This inspired no negative comment; the Axis had been the aggressors and the defeated states deserved to be excluded from international affairs until fascist and ultranationalist influences were eliminated from their domestic politics. As the monstrous character of Nazi rule over invaded areas and Germany itself became clearer over the summer of 1945, fascism acquired such bad odor that anti-fascism appeared to provide a common rallying point for the member states. However, the consensus that being anti-fascist meant being "democratic" and "peace-loving" was too thin to disguise for long the varying meanings attached to those terms by different governments or avert the normal erosion of alliances once acute danger had passed.

Great-power consensus

Confidence in a better future rested heavily on beliefs that the great powers would maintain their wartime collaboration despite differences in ideology and interest. Britain, the Soviet Union, and the United States had collaborated successfully during the war; China and France – added to the ranks of permanent members of the Security Council out of respect for their past and likely future role in the international system – were expected to increase their roles now that they were free of Axis invaders. Though the French declined to join the other four in co-sponsoring the San Francisco Conference, they did attend and supported the main features of Franklin Roosevelt's vision of the great powers as "global policemen" maintaining order on behalf of the wider community. Latin American governments expressed considerable unhappiness with the policemen idea,[3] and delegations of some other smaller powers also raised objections. Faced with the insistence by the "Big 5" on their initial design, the others backed away and accepted both the division of labor between the Security Council and the General Assembly, and the special veto privileges of the "Big 5" in the Council.

Functionalism

The goals of the anti-Axis alliance had consistently included creation of a democratic postwar order spreading economic prosperity, education, and other social benefits widely. Political elites and ordinary citizens alike believed that the economic distress and social tensions caused by the Great Depression had facilitated the rise of fascism. Though believing that global socialist revolution was the only sure cure for economic and social problems, the Soviet bloc did not interfere with establishment of the international-level Functionalism that complemented the Keynesian doctrines of national macroeconomic management widely accepted in the West. Though declining to participate in some activities, including the Bretton Woods institutions, it did join most of the Specialized Agencies.

Gradual decolonization

The process of decolonization had begun before 1945, with grants of independence to the League "Class A" Mandates of Syria, Iraq, and Transjordan, the US decision to carry out a phased transition to Philippine independence, and the wartime British promise of independence to India. What a later British Prime Minister, Harold Macmillan, called the "winds of change"[4] had already begun to rise as nationalism among colonial peoples and strengthened anti-imperial sentiments among Europeans and Americans converged to create broad consensus on the idea that all peoples had an equal right to self-determination. The UN Charter anticipated a continuation of this process, both by extending the Trusteeship System (its version of the League Mandates) to include colonies taken from Japan in 1945, and by specifying rules that would apply to all non-self-governing territories in Chapter XI. While the Trusteeship Council supervised administration of the colonies formally designated as Trust Territories, Chapter XI and Charter invocations of the right of self-determination gave the General Assembly ample tools for prodding colonial powers to dissolve their empires.

In 1945, the Soviets were already trying to hasten the pace of decolonization by emphasizing the right of self-determination and equating it with political independence. They pushed to secure references to "the principle of equal rights and self-determination of peoples" in Articles 1 and 55 of the Charter. They also consistently interpreted "self-determination" to mean independence and stated repeatedly that they hoped to see an early end to colonialism. However, the outline of a gradual process was incorporated into the parts of the Charter dealing with colonial areas. Article 73 enjoined states administering colonies to "recognize the principle that the interests of the inhabitants of these territories are paramount" and "to develop self-government, to take into account of the political aspirations of the peoples, and to assist them in the progressive development of their free political institutions, according to the particular circumstances of each territory and its peoples and their varying stages of advancement." Article 76 enjoined states administering Trust Territories to "promote the political, economic, social, and educational advancement of the inhabitants of the trust territories, and their progressive development towards self-government or independence as may be appropriate to the particular circumstances of each territory and its peoples and the freely expressed wishes of the peoples concerned."

Whether done gradually, as the Western powers expected, or rapidly, as the Soviets wanted, accepting decolonization as a goal meant undertaking to transform the international system. Most obviously, eliminating colonial rule would mean abolishing one form of imperialism. It would also entail moving beyond the highly Europe-centered international order of the League and early UN era to a more global order in which other cultural traditions would be asserted. Full decolonization would also complete the transition to an international system where the internal and external legitimacy of states rested on organization as nation-states, political communities based on a population's sense that it constitutes a particular people determining its own political future.[5]

The Cold War

Impact of East–West ideological competition

The renewal of ideological competition between Leninist planned-economy states and liberal democratic market-economy states soon split the wartime alliance into Eastern and Western blocs, and created a rather different world than foreseen at the San Francisco Conference. All parts of the UN system, including the General Assembly, were strained by the changes and developed in ways unanticipated as the UN was being shaped.

Revival of the ideological competition, which had begun with the Russian Revolution in 1917, took some people by surprise but ought to have been expected from the generally sour relations prevailing between Western powers and the Soviet Union during the 1920s and 1930s. The doctrinal basis of their ideological differences remained, even though the Western European states had increased the level of state direction of the economy and the USA had shifted away from strongly *laissez-faire* policies to greater macroeconomic management during the New Deal. However, the new ideological competition played out differently. The Second World War elimination of fascism meant that ideological competition was two-, rather than three-, sided while changes in distribution of material capability revealed and enhanced by the war had yielded a bipolar rather than a multipolar international system. These two simplifications gave to Soviet–Western ideological competition a focus and intensity that had been blurred before 1945.

The General Assembly lacked authority to resolve this ideological contention, which would have to be worked out within and between member states. However, it provided a forum where each bloc could project its ideological vision, criticize the other's ideological vision, and appeal for support among the neutral states. Except on occasions when the two blocs happened to agree (usually for rather different reasons) on some particular course of action, UN bodies – including the General Assembly – were frozen into inaction on Cold War-related issues. The impact of ideological competition was evident in the long and difficult process of moving from the Universal Declaration of Human Rights (adopted over Soviet bloc opposition in 1948) to the International Covenants on Civil and Political Rights, and on Economic, Social and Cultural Rights, completed only in 1961. Stalemate even extended to the question of admitting additional member states: after increasing from 51 to 60 states in 1950, further admissions were stymied until 1955 because each bloc resisted admitting states endorsed by the other.

Superpower ideological conflict was paralleled by political–military rivalry. Having built into the UN collective security system the "circuit breaker" of great-power vetoes in the Security Council, the superpowers each resorted to the older devices of military alliances with friendly governments and informal patron–client relations with like-minded factions in other countries. Yet the alliances took on different character during the Cold War. The main ones – the North Atlantic Treaty Organization (NATO) and the Warsaw Pact – were institutionalized in multilateral form and made consistent at least in name with the UN collective security system by establishing them as mechanisms for the collective self-defense of all alliance partners. The net result in Europe was stalemate, a forty-five-year-long division of that continent where UN bodies had no significant role in the conduct or outcome of the superpower rivalry. Though such a result could be interpreted as consistent with Article 107 of the Charter, which specifically excluded UN involvement in defining or amending the peace settlement imposed on the Axis, the superpowers' shared reluctance to bring European issues to the world body was the main constraint limiting UN activity on that continent.

Even though Japan was also covered by the Charter strictures on enemy states, UN bodies were more involved in Asian affairs. The Chinese Civil War, and communist victory in 1949, created a more fluid situation marked by bilateral alliances and considerable bloc probing in areas not firmly attached to either side. The US-led coalition's invocation of the United Nations collective security system to prevent North Korea from taking over South Korea was the fortuitous exception to the rule that UN activity on political questions was confined to decolonization or mediation efforts. The Soviet government, which was boycotting the Security Council to protest the US-led majority's refusal to seat Chinese communist delegates as representatives of China, learned a hard lesson and quickly returned to the council, forcing the improvisation of General Assembly leadership under Resolution 377(V). Yet the stalemate on the battlefield provided India and other Asian states with the opportunity to nudge the UN into a mediatory role in Korea more consistent with the form of UN activity elsewhere in Asia.

The US-led coalition did not attempt again to bypass the Security Council by invoking the Uniting for Peace procedure. It did, however, continue to use the General Assembly to register verbal condemnation of Soviet actions like suppression of the Hungarian revolt in October 1956. The Soviets were less successful in securing direct condemnations of the USA, but had begun to perceive that the growth of neutral and Nonaligned sentiment would soon make the assembly a more congenial place for their efforts to win over opinion in other parts of the world.

Effect on UN consideration of economic issues

The Cold War also inspired a redirection of UN economic and social activity. Originally UN agencies were expected to have a significant role in reconstruction of those areas of Europe and Asia most devastated by the Second World War. This was reflected in the naming of the International Bank for Reconstruction and Development at the 1944 Bretton Woods Conference and in establishment of the UN Relief and Rehabilitation Agency (UNRAA) in 1943 even before the Charter was drafted. UNRRA provided considerable assistance, 70 percent of it derived from US government or private funds. This ended when the United States Congress, perceiving that UNRRA work in Eastern Europe was helping prop up the new Leninist regimes there, cut off US funding and the agency was dissolved in June 1947. Later US reconstruction aid was channeled through the Marshall Plan, where Congress could exercise greater supervision over its use, and the Soviet bloc developed its own mechanisms for postwar reconstruction.

With postwar reconstruction removed from their agendas, UN bodies were left to consider broader economic questions. This had been anticipated in the Charter, particularly in the second preambular paragraph commitment that member states would "employ international machinery for the promotion of the economic and social advancement of all peoples." The Cold War simply meant that these discussions took center stage at the UN earlier than anticipated. As an Afro-Asian bloc consisting mainly of newly independent states began to congeal, they reinforced the Latin American desire to have UN bodies address economic development and the needs of nonindustrial countries.

In the late 1940s and early 1950s, both East and West believed that fairly simple policy measures would yield economic development. Soviet bloc governments believed that development would follow when capitalism (markets plus private ownership of means of production) was abolished, economic inequality ended through state confiscation of the land and capital assets previously held by capitalists, and the whole economy organized through central planning. Western bloc governments believed that development would follow when countries embarked on "modernization," using the machinery of the state to break up traditional patterns of activity, build physical infrastructure, provide modern education, and – if need be – build and operate state-owned enterprises in leading sectors. Though the exact programs suggested by British Fabians, Western European social democrats, and American development economists varied in detail, all converged on a broad vision of state-led economic and social change to be fostered through mass mobilization and considerable state initiative in promoting economic activity. In all these visions, the Functionalist doctrines guiding the UN specialized agencies needed to be supplemented by provision of material assistance in the forms of finance (loans, grants) and technical aid (dispatch of experts to train local officials or technical personnel).

Outside the Soviet bloc, which defined capitalism as the main obstacle to development, the main challenge to "conventional" development economists' emphasis on change at the national level was the structuralist analysis of Raul Prebisch and his followers in Latin America. This analysis argued that developing countries' prospects were severely limited by the existing global division of economic activity. Nonindustrial states, producing mainly raw materials and agricultural products, would find it difficult to industrialize because constantly deteriorating terms of trade prevented them from earning the sums needed to start modern industrial enterprises. Prebisch's analysis attributed those deteriorating terms of trade to a combination of steadily increasing prices for industrial goods and steadily decreasing prices for the raw materials and agricultural commodities typically produced by Third World countries. Industrialization, in this view, would require de-linking from international trade and relying on state mobilization of internal resources.

Though the structuralist explanation, and its alternate policy prescription of "development from inside" (also called "import substitution industrialization"), was attractive to many Latin American economists, politicians, and intellectuals, it was only weakly reflected in most United Nations discussions in the 1950s. Though Prebisch headed and could use the UN Economic Commission for Latin America to publicize the analysis, General Assembly and Economic and Social Council discussions focused more on the need to create additional multilateral lending and technical assistance mechanisms to supplement bilateral and World Bank aid programs.

Developing countries' agitation for directing greater UN effort towards development began to meet success in the mid-1950s as both superpowers identified "the underdeveloped countries" as key addressees in their global ideological competition. The Afro-Asian group, perceiving the advantages of being courted by both superpowers, began coalescing into a distinct bloc of their own starting at the 1955 Bandung Conference. Formal establishment of the Nonaligned Movement in 1961 increased their collective influence, reinforcing the willingness of the new Kennedy administration in the USA to expand US foreign aid programs and support establishing the first of four UN "Development Decades" in 1961. Though the goals for aid levels and economic growth were not met, the Decades began the pattern of whole-membership discussion of development issues and establishment of broad goals that persists today.

The Cold War and decolonization

Agitation among colonial populations to pick up the pace of decolonization received a powerful boost from the superpower competition for influence in the emerging Third World. Both superpowers were firmly committed to ending colonialism, but still disagreed about timing. The Soviets enjoyed some political advantage since Imperial Russia had not engaged in over-ocean colonialism. Stalin had maintained hold of most of the tsarist empire, but used a more subtle approach in organizing the post-1945 extension of Soviet control into Eastern Europe. States in the region were left formally independent but managed closely through local communist parties following Moscow's direction. In contrast, several members of the Western bloc were colonial powers. While the European powers' political and economic power did not depend heavily on continued possession of colonies, important segments of governmental and public opinion remained attached to holding on after 1945. The domestic politics of the issue in the West became more complicated with the Cold War, as many Western conservatives came to regard Third World nationalism as controlled or readily co-opted by communists and many liberals regarded continuing colonialism as increasing local receptivity to communist appeals.

Assembly majorities began more active efforts to hasten decolonization after 16 newly independent African states were admitted to the UN in 1960. The Declaration on the Granting of Independence to Colonial Countries and Peoples[5] endorsed a near-equation of self-determination of peoples with existence as an independent state. The Fourth Committee and a new standing committee on decolonization, the Special Committee on Implementation of the Declaration on the Granting of Independence to Colonial Countries and Peoples, issued constant verbal condemnations of colonialism and colonial powers. Yet, contrary to the perceptions of right-wing groups and parties in the West, Nonaligned and Soviet bloc positions were not identical. The Soviets typically pressed for more immediate action than all but the most radical of the Nonaligned were prepared to support, but this was often missed because the moderates shaped the resolutions while the radicals dominated the debates.

Arab–Israeli conflict

The conflict over who should live where and under what political arrangements in the geographical area covered by the League of Nations Mandate over Palestine has absorbed more General Assembly energy and attention over a longer time than any other political issue. Though in many respects a question of decolonization, it developed a unique momentum and durability because of the depth of disagreement among the populations on the ground. The conflict emerged in the 1930s as both Arabs and Jews living in the area sorted out their visions of a political future while the other Middle Eastern areas placed in League Class A Mandates were moving towards independence. Articulate Arab opinion opposed the Zionist vision of a separate Jewish state. While many Jews in the area, both the long-settled and the more recent arrivals, supported the Zionist goal of an independent Jewish state, others held to socialist visions of a binational workers' state created as Arab and Jewish workers united against local economic elites.[7] The British, trying to steer between the two populations, began floating partition plans in 1937 but could not secure agreement from both Arabs and Jews to any of them.

When the Second World War ended, the British found themselves where they had been in the 1930s: eager to end the Mandate but wanting to secure agreement between the local Arab and Jewish populations on the political future of the area before they withdrew. The Jews sought to increase immigration to the point that the Jewish community, which was 11 percent of the population in 1922,[7] would be self-sustaining and able to defend itself. The Arabs sought to ensure limitations on Jewish immigration and land purchases so that the Zionist vision could not be imposed. Hardliners on both sides made it difficult to formulate any mutually acceptable arrangements.

The General Assembly got involved in the postwar effort to define such an arrangement when the British referred the matter to it in September 1947. In the Ad hoc Committee on Palestine established to handle the issue, Arab member states strongly opposed partition. Stalin, setting aside his strong anti-Semitism for the moment, put Soviet influence behind partition. After considerable negotiating and pressuring among the members, the General Assembly endorsed a partition plan establishing separate Arab and Jewish states, and placing the common capital of Jerusalem under international administration, by a vote of 39 in favor to 13 against with 10 abstentions. In the following plenary debates, the US government briefly proposed establishing a UN trusteeship over Palestine, a sudden reversal causing dismay both inside US policy-making circles and at the UN. Though appealing to some Arabs, the prospect of trusteeship was not attractive to the Zionists, who saw partition as an endorsement of their plans and trusteeship as likely to frustrate them.

All the while, everyone involved in the assembly discussion realized that tensions in the area were high. Both Arab and Jewish armed groups were ready to fight, and the latter were violently harassing the British administration. The British precipitated the first crisis in late 1947 by announcing their intention to withdraw their forces and administrators on 14 May 1948, a move intended to get the local populations to settle down into serious discussions by setting a deadline. Though the US government opposed establishment of a large UN force to maintain order, the superpowers and the rest of the UN membership did accept that some UN role was needed and created the UN Truce Supervision Organization in April 1948. When the British did withdraw on 14 May, the Zionists declared the independence of Israel. The contingent alignment of the superpowers persisted, with both the Soviet and US governments recognizing the state of Israel later that day.

Egyptian, Lebanese, Syrian, Iraqi, and Jordanian forces attacked Zionist-held areas, but despite larger numbers failed to prevail. By the time armistices were arranged in 1949, Israel held about 75 percent of Mandate Palestine, more than allocated to them under the 1947 partition plan. Egypt took a strip running from Gaza to its own border, Israel and Jordan split Jerusalem between themselves; and Jordan annexed the rest of the Mandate area.

The seeds of later rounds of conflict were planted at this time. The Israelis did not allow Arabs who had fled Jewish-held areas during the fighting to return to their original abodes. The Arab states insisted that the displaced Arabs should be allowed to return to their homes, and treated them as refugees to be housed rather than immigrants to be integrated into society. The Jewish population of Israel continued to rise, owing in significant part to immigration from Middle Eastern countries where life was becoming uncomfortable for Jews. Arab public opinion and Arab governments were extremely unhappy – with the fact Israel existed, with the *de facto* boundaries between Israeli and Palestinian areas, with the large-scale expulsions of Arabs from Israeli-controlled areas, and with the wide international recognition of Israel's existence.

Parallel Security Council and General Assembly efforts to get partition back on track stalled. Stalemate persisted on the question of whether displaced Arabs could return to their pre-May 1948 abodes. Arab governments continued to insist on an unconditional right of return. Israeli worries that they would become a fifth column in any renewed fighting were kept sharp by Arab governments' refusal to recognize Israel's existence or terminate the state of war they had declared in 1948, reinforcing the Zionist hardliners' rejection of return. Stalemate, low-intensity fighting, UN truce supervision, and UN mediation efforts continued, but what was now generally known as the Arab–Israeli conflict did not inspire focused international attention again until the Suez Crisis of October 1956.

Concerned by the continuing state of war and Egyptian sponsorship of cross-border raids, the Israeli government joined with the British and French in armed intervention against Egypt in October 1956. The British and French used the occasion of Nasser's nationalization of the Suez Canal – itself Nasser's reaction to a US decision against lending money for the Aswan High Dam project – to try overthrowing the increasingly neutralist, pan-Arabist, and therefore very irritating Nasser. However, the intervention bogged down and Nasser's position was strengthened. Each seeking to court Third World opinion, the superpowers again joined momentarily in condemning the British and French intervention, and supporting UN efforts to hasten British and French withdrawal from Egypt. Yet their positions regarding Israel diverged, with the Soviets beginning to move towards greater support of the Arab side in the conflict. However, a majority of the UN membership agreed that Israeli action was justified by Egyptian provocations, and linked Israeli withdrawal to the pre-1956 lines with an augmented UN involvement in the UN Emergency Force (UNEF) ultimately deployed only along the Egyptian side of the border.

The conflict then reverted to its earlier form of local Arabs versus the Jewish population with formation of Palestinian political movements. The Arab League acknowledged the shift and sought to increase its effectiveness by creating the Palestine Liberation Organization in 1964. Though in fact under Egyptian control, the PLO's existence increased the pressure on Nasser to prove his claims to leadership of the Arab world by doing something decisive about the Arab–Israeli conflict. Palestinians began attacking within Israel, and the Israeli government reacted by retaliating against Jordan in early 1967. Spurred by rumors that Israel intended to attack Syria as well, Nasser prepared a direct attack. This required asking the UN to withdraw UNEF, which gave the Israelis ample time to prepare for large-scale war. The Israelis launched pre-emptive attacks on 5 June that caught the Egyptian air force on the ground. Within a few days, to the surprise of everyone except themselves, Israeli forces occupied Sinai as far as the Suez Canal, part of southern Syria (the Golan Heights), the Jordanian-occupied part of Mandate Palestine (the West Bank), and all of Jerusalem.

Diplomacy at the UN was complicated by the fact that the superpowers were now clearly aligned on opposite sides, and willing to act in concert only to prevent spread of war or too severe a defeat for their own client. The Third World was also divided, with most African and Asian governments ready to follow the Arab states' lead, but the Latin Americans seeking a middle ground.[9]

Anticipating US vetoes of its proposals to require unconditional Israeli withdrawal from the areas they had just occupied, the Soviets invoked the "Uniting for Peace" procedure to shift discussion into an emergency assembly session. It began on 17 June, and quickly bogged down. In mid-July, the Latin American group tried to break the stalemate. It proposed that Israeli forces be withdrawn to the territory they occupied before the June War, that all states in the area end belligerency so that every state in the Middle East can enjoy their "rightful freedom" from threat of war, and have the UN – through the Security Council – work with the parties to deal with all aspects of the situation, including refugees and transit rights in international waterways. When Arab governments rejected any direct reference to ending belligerency, the superpowers agreed on the less direct phrasing "renunciation of all claims and acts inconsistent with" states' rights to maintain themselves and live in peace with neighbors. Despite Soviet urgings, the Arab governments also declined this formulation. Discussion then shifted back to the Security Council, and in September the assembly's emergency session was ended without adopting any resolutions.

In the Security Council, the superpowers took up the proposals they had hammered out during the assembly discussions. Security Council Resolution 242 defined a linked peace plan: the Israelis should withdraw to the areas they held before the war while the Arab states should end their state of war and recognize the right of all states in the area to live in peace. UN mediation and the UN Truce Supervision Organization (but not UNEF) continued, but yet again negotiations stalled and the conflict was left to fester.

South–North contention over the international economic order

By the mid-1960s it was obvious that economic development in the Third World was more difficult than anticipated in the 1940s. Prebisch's structuralist approach was gaining adherents outside Latin America, particularly in Africa where economic growth was also very slow. Two streams of academic analysis, world-system theory and dependency theory, further elaborated the basic structuralist proposition that organizing the international economy on open-market principles systematically favors the industrial states and is itself the main cause of "underdevelopment." These newer academic analyses fit comfortably with, and drew in varying degrees on, Marxist theories of imperialism, which also attributed the problems of developing countries to their subordinate place in a global capitalist economy.

The emphasis on state planning and co-ordination

In the 1960s and 1970s the common structuralist and Marxist belief that extensive state management of the economy, whether through nationalizing major areas of economic activity or through comprehensive central planning, provided a superior path to development than reliance on private enterprise and market economics appeared confirmed in the real world. Soviet economic expansion continued at a rate making credible Soviet Premier Nikita Khrushchev's 1960 boast to US Vice President Nixon that "we will bury you." Maoist visions of a primarily rural and agricultural economy moving into the industrial era by establishing industrial operations in villages, the basis of the Great Leap Forward campaign, had not yet been discredited. By the late 1960s, the long and ultimately unsuccessful US involvement in Southeast Asia had alienated considerable segments of public opinion in the USA and Western Europe, and helped encourage development of a widespread "counterculture" among younger people in the industrial countries. Though mild compared to the post-1973 recession, economic slowdown in the late 1960s seemed to confirm analyses stressing the weaknesses of Western economies.

Statist challenges to the Keynsian "embedded liberalism" of the postwar international economic order[10] rose as the UN membership continued to increase. Close observers of UN politics could see that the US-led majority in the General Assembly was no longer in firm control, and this became obvious to even the casual observer during the long stalemate over peacekeeping expenses in 1964–5 (see Chapter 4). The 24 Latin Americans were now over-shadowed by the seventy-strong Afro-Asian bloc, but finding common cause with it on economic issues. Cold War competition between the superpowers continued, but was now complicated by the simultaneous competition for influence in communist parties and other Marxist movements between the Soviet Union, with its Leninist urban proletariat-oriented emphasis, and China, with its Maoist vision of revolution in the countryside spreading to engulf the cities. Though the People's Republic did not assume China's seat in UN bodies until September 1971, the Albanian delegation acted as its proxy in the 1960s and brought the Sino-Soviet rift into the General Assembly.[11] Faced was being outflanked from the left, the Soviets simultane-ously pursued political *détente* with the West, provided strong verbal support for the most radical Third World propositions on issues of decolonization and organizing the international economy, and sought influence in Marxist move-ments around the world.

Early Third World successes

Though global economic growth was slowing down, the early to mid-1960s were still a period of Western optimism in which the problem of production seemed solved and issues of distribution could take center stage internation-ally as well as domestically. The new Third World majority in the General Assembly was able to exert sufficient pressure on the Western industrial states to secure special concessions to developing countries in GATT and some additional UN and World Bank aid programs. Efforts to create a large new UN development program failed, but the assembly resolution convening a UN Conference on Trade and Development (UNCTAD) for 1964 set discussion in a structuralist direction by emphasizing the need to establish a "new division of labor with new patterns of production and trade."[12] Though the most ambitious structuralist ideas and the most ambi-tious Third World proposals for new UN bodies were not adopted at that conference, the Third World majority won agreement to establishing UNCTAD as a periodic conference with a permanent secretariat headed by Raul Prebisch. However, the scanty results of the 1964 talks demonstrated that demands for major changes in international economic regimes would not gain serious attention unless and until developing countries acquired economic leverage over the West.

Such leverage appeared to have been acquired in 1973, when Arab members of the Organization of Petroleum Exporting Countries (OPEC) used their recently won control over oil multinationals' operations on their territory to impose an oil embargo on the USA and Western Europe in the aftermath of the 1973 Arab–Israeli war. The oil embargo revealed the extreme sensitivity of energy markets and emboldened OPEC producers to quadruple the price of crude oil. The oil multinationals had no particular reason to resist because they could simply pass the increase on to their customers. A few voices in the West did propose using military force to impose a rollback, but most public and governmental opinion rejected that solution.

"Commodity power" and the NIEO

Though oil-importing developing countries suffered even more from the price hikes and ensuing global economic recession than the industrial countries, OPEC was a source of great inspiration for the governments of developing countries. Producers of other commodities were confident that forming cartels, or merely threatening to form cartels, would secure Western acceptance of increased prices for their own products. For a brief period of time, in a mood exemplified by the slogan "one, two, many OPECs,"[13] developing countries firmly believed they had acquired the economic leverage necessary to make the Western industrial countries accept thorough restructuring of the international economy.

The optimism of developing countries was manifest in the demands for creation of a New International Economic Order (NIEO) issued at the Nonaligned's 1973 Algiers summit. In the General Assembly, the G-77 pressed successfully for accelerating the schedule of special-assembly sessions on international economic issues. To the special session on Development and International Economic Co-operation scheduled for 1975 was added a separate special session on Raw Materials and Development in spring 1974. Setting the agendas for these sessions involved intense contention because industrial countries wanted to include discussion of energy prices while the Group of 77 rejected that idea lest its always-precarious unity be disturbed.

The special sessions marked the peak of G-77 optimism about the prospects of securing a transformation of international economic regimes. Third World countries were still buoyed by OPEC's success, recession-inspired economic pessimism and counterculture rejection of "materialism" and "consumerism" reduced Western confidence, and the Soviets were seeking to avoid being outflanked from the left by the Chinese by supporting the most radical Third World ideas. Led by Algeria and others of its most statist wing, the Group of 77 came to the special sessions demanding a comprehensive restructuring of the international economy. It hoped to 1) redistribute financial resources, 2) alter the terms of trade through commodity agreements ensuring stabilized or (better yet) increased prices for commodities, 3) shift industrial activity from North to South through a set of negotiated allocations of productive capacity among countries, and 4) shift the locus of international economic decision-making to existing or new multilateral forums where developing countries would have at least equal say with industrial ones in decision-making.[14]

It is a measure of the times that even US Secretary of State Henry Kissinger, renowned for his unconcern with economic issues, paid serious attention and agreed that some concessions were needed. However, what he and other Western leaders were prepared to accept fell far short of what Algeria and other G-77 leaders desired. Unable to attain Western acceptance of their ambitious program of restructuring, but needing to maintain a long list of demands addressing its own members' concerns by adding them all together, the G-77's leaders forged on with the coalition they could recruit. The Declaration on the Establishment of a New International Economic Order was adopted "without objection" and the Charter of Economic Rights and Duties of States by a vote of 120 to 6 with 10 abstentions.[15] Though major Western states were among the objectors and abstainers, the G-77 was confident that they could be persuaded or pressured into agreement.

Both resolutions were phrased in highly abstract terms, and their elaboration was to be the subject of follow-on "global negotiations" ("global" indicating both the breadth of the agenda and the selection of participants). These were to be sponsored by or occur in the General Assembly, to maximize both G-77 voting power and ability to make issue-linkages. Confident of its leverage, and of their moral claims for redistribution as recompense for past and current wrongs, the G-77 leadership held out for maximalist demands. It kept its coalition together through adding all members' desires together and invoking the need for Third World solidarity to rally doubters.

Receding of the NIEO tide

None of the follow-up efforts – the twenty-seven-nation Conference on International Economic Co-operation (1975–7), the all-inclusive General Assembly Committee of the Whole (1978–80), or the Assembly's 11th Special Session on the NIEO (1981) – yielded significant results. There was a brief interlude of renewed optimism in 1980 when both Western and OPEC governments relented on agenda issues and agreed to address the whole range of economic issues – development, debt, financial aid, commodities, and energy at the 11th Special Session. However, this faded rapidly as the essential stalemate between a G-77 seeking to give the assembly co-ordinating authority over all UN bodies, including GATT and the Bretton Woods institutions, came up against Western – particularly US, British, and West German – refusal to accept any such assembly role. Thus the 11th Special Session ended without adoption of anything comparable to the NIEO resolutions of the mid-1970s.

The potential for drawing in the more resistant industrial states faded for several reasons. First, though the 1979 oil price spike triggered by the Iranian revolution temporarily deepened the global recession, its rapid reversal as supplies quickly returned to normal further demonstrated the hollowness of "commodity power." Second, economic beliefs in the West were beginning to shift. While most Western states remained committed to some form of redistributive economics domestically and internationally, the counterculture was weakening and a new "neoliberal" economics – emphasizing reliance on market mechanisms, private enterprise, and reduction of government regulatory and redistributive programs – was taken up by newly elected leaders in Britain and the USA. Third, despite efforts to rework positions in 1980–1, G-77 positions continued to be marked by considerable rigidity because the members' diverging economic interests were reconcilable only by developing package positions that offered something for each and omitted anything objectionable to any significant subgrouping.

The meager results of the 11th Special Session intensified discussion within the Group of 77 about what to do next. Some advocated shifting primary attention to increasing South–South co-operation. The notion of "de-linking" from the global economy remained popular among Third World leaders and policy analysts, and South–South co-operation suggested a way that countries too small to pursue autarkic economic policies alone could de-link by joining a wider group. De-linking was also a major goal of the contemporaneous simultaneous demands for a New World Information and Communications Order that would allow countries to protect themselves from the "cultural imperialism" borne by Western media and entertainment.

The Palestinian–Israeli conflict

The most significant results of the 1967 War were Arab desire to erase the humiliation of defeat and a significant increase in the number of Palestinian Arabs under Israeli rule. Though Nasser remained the link between Palestinians and other Arab states until his death in 1970, initiative soon passed a more autonomous PLO. On the surface, the 1973 War revived the pattern of neighboring Arab states taking the lead, but co-ordination among them and with the PLO was deeper this time. Under Anwar Sadat's more careful planning, Egyptian and Syrian forces attacked Israel in the Sinai and the Golan Heights respectively on 6 October. The Israelis mounted counter-attacks on the 9th and 14th, regaining the ground they had lost, then advancing towards Damascus and encircling Egyptian forces in the Sinai. The superpowers, seeking to prevent defeat of their client and major confrontation with each other, used the Security Council to impose a ceasefire and expanded UN monitoring.

The 1973 War did not change the actual allocation of territory, but the better performance of Arab armed forces altered perceptions of the regional balance of power. OPEC's oil embargo weapon was effective in securing greater diplomatic isolation of Israel by putting pressure on Japan to move away from supporting Israeli positions and increasing the already-evident Western European tendency to support self-determination for the Palestinians. Politics in the Security Council, where Resolution 242 remained the lodestar, were not seriously affected because of the mutually balancing US and Soviet vetoes. The balance did shift in the assembly where the radical African and Arab governments came to lead the Nonaligned, the Japanese and Western Europeans became increasingly critical of Israeli policy, and the Latin Americans also shifted towards the Palestinian side. The new situation was manifest in the cordial treatment accorded to PLO Chairman Yasir Arafat when he addressed the assembly in 1974 and adoption of the "Zionism is a form of racism" resolution by a vote of 72 to 35 with 32 abstentions in 1975.[16] This put the assembly on record as removing Zionist aspirations from the accepted category of nationalism and consigning them to the worst classification in the Nonaligned lexicon.

The resolution had two wider political effects. First, it firmly committed the assembly to one side in the conflict, hardening Israeli refusal to deal with the UN. Second, coming as it did at the height of Third World radicalism on decolonization and development issues, it had strong reverberations in the policy debates of both superpowers. The Soviets read it as another sign that the "correlation of forces" around the world was shifting in their favor. The US neoconservatives were confirmed in their view that the assembly was a "dangerous place" in which the USA should re-engage the ideological struggle, and their arguments won wider hearing among the public.

South–North/East–West

Soviet reassertion and strong US response

The early to mid-1970s were a period of apparent *détente* between the super-powers. Below the surface, however, the momentum for a new round of confrontation was building. In the mid-1970s the Soviets had several reasons to believe that time was ripe for a greater push and a reintensification of Cold War competition in the Third World. Global recession, the Vietnam War-induced shattering of the foreign policy consensus in the USA, the "youth revolt" and "counterculture," and the apparent increase in Western European distancing from the USA appeared to have sapped Western strength. Continuing Soviet military build-up and Soviet bloc successes in supporting leftist regimes in various parts of the Third World suggested that the moment was right for new initiatives. Ideological challenge from China also receded (though geopolitical contention remained high) when Mao Zedong died in September 1976 and his radical immediate successors the "Gang of Four" were displaced in early 1977.

Soviet optimism was increased by developments within the Nonaligned. The Cubans succeeded in capturing the leadership, and chaired the Nonaligned from 1976 until 1979. The Cubans used Nonaligned meetings to advance their proposition that the Soviet Union, as a socialist country that had never practiced colonialism or extracted any wealth from developing countries, was the "natural ally" of the Third World. For their part, the Soviets found it relatively easy to substantiate Cuban claims by supporting Third World positions in the General Assembly and other UN bodies.

Though the Carter administration had begun to adopt a stiffer policy after the Soviet intervention in Afghanistan, it was swept aside in the 1980 election and replaced by the far more confrontational Reagan administration. Several of its policies alienated Western European and Third World opinion and fed the Soviet propaganda mills. US intervention in Nicaragua against the Sandinistas, involving assistance to the local "contra" opposition and direct US attacks on and minelaying in three Nicaraguan harbors, was unpopular around the world. US intervention in Grenada, though eventually supported by other governments in the region, added to the negative impressions of the US. The Reagan Strategic Defense Initiative (known to domestic and foreign opponents alike as the "Star Wars" program) aroused considerable criticisms both domestically and in Western Europe, giving the Soviets plenty of opportunity to portray the US as the country most determined to frustrate disarmament efforts.

Yet Soviet activities were also the subject of international criticism. Soviet support for Vietnamese intervention in Cambodia to overthrow the Khmer Rouge and substitute a communist regime more to Hanoi's liking triggered a long refusal to accept the new regime as the government of Cambodia (see Chapter 4). Criticism of the Soviets might have faded as others paid more attention to the contentions among Cambodian factions, but their intervention in Afghanistan to help one communist faction take control of the government from another and then maintain power in the face of guerrilla resistance elicited wider and longer-lasting disfavor.

US neoconservatives, seeing the more radical elements of the Nonaligned and the Soviet bloc as a stable controling majority steering the assembly, urged the Reagan administration to "go into opposition" and make clear that the USA was no longer willing to ignore assembly condemnations or support certain UN programs. They missed the assembly's equal readiness to condemn Soviet interventions, but were more on the mark in noticing that the Third World majority shielded its own members from criticism and continued to follow rejectionist Arab leadership on issues relating to Israel and Palestine.

Yet, in one of many historical ironies, the late 1970s and early 1980s were the moment when Soviet internal decline accelerated. The Soviet dissident Andrei Amalrik, who asked "will the Soviet Union survive until 1984?" attracted a brief flurry of attention in the late 1970s, but few Western observers believed that the Soviet Union would fall apart in their lifetimes.[17] Leonid Brezhnev, who allowed personal corruption to soar to heights unseen under communist rule, presided over an increasingly inefficient and technologically stumbling Soviet economy and a gradual erosion of belief in Leninism.

Erosion of Third World confidence in a statist NIEO

Even without awareness of the depth of Soviet economic stagnation or downturn, opponents of the NIEO gained confidence through the early and mid-1980s. Oil shortages soon gave way to oil gluts and lower prices as fuel substitution and energy conservation in industrial states changed the contours of the global energy market. OPEC members now faced the problem of restricting supply sufficiently to limit the slide of prices. This was more difficult because many of the members were committed to ambitious and expensive development programs that encouraged cheating on mutually agreed production limits to increase revenues. The vision of a world of commodity producer cartels faded away as it proved even more difficult to maintain collusive arrangements on other products.

Supporters of state-directed economics were chastened and supporters of market economics emboldened as the extent of Soviet economic decline became apparent. Soviet economists had noticed the decline prior to Leonid Brezhnev's death in November 1982, but their warnings were unheeded. Later, and particularly after Mikhail Gorbachev became Communist Party General Secretary in March 1985, information about Soviet economic stagnation circulated more widely in and outside the country. Soviet citizens and the more perceptive Soviet leaders and policy advisers did not need the new set of data to realize that their country was falling behind technologically. They could see it by comparing goods manufactured domestically with those imported from other parts of the world. By 1983, Soviet specialists on Third World economies were advising that developing countries should become more involved in, rather than isolate themselves from, international trade and investment.[18] The Chinese, under the less ideological leadership that succeeded the "Gang of Four" in 1977, also noted Soviet experience and began their experiments with partial adoption of market mechanisms and private enterprise.

More telling for members of the Group of 77, and noticed by increasing numbers of them in the early 1980s, was the significant difference in economic performance between the Southeast Asian "Tigers" emphasizing land reform and export-led growth, and countries emphasizing import substitution industrialization plus insulation from world markets. While academic analysts found many reasons for the divergence of economic performance among developing countries, the combination of Soviet stagnation and high East-Asian growth made market economics more attractive in the Third World than it had been at any time since 1945.

Thus, by the mid-1980s prospects of adopting the highly state-centered NIEO design for international economic regimes had almost disappeared. Western opposition was not confined to, though was most forcefully expressed by, the British and US governments. Even the USSR and China were backing away from their rhetorical backing. Soviet economists were already advising Third World countries that "de-linking" would yield them little economic benefit. Third World governments were cognizant that limited aid and trade, and their outmoded technology, meant that establishing economic ties with the Soviets carried limited benefit.[19] The Chinese leadership embarked on an ambitious program of economic reform converting China from a fully planned to a mixed economy by opening up selected sectors to local and private enterprise. Many developing countries, particularly the oil-importers, remained mired in the debt they had run up in the 1970s, and were forced to deal more with the Bretton Woods institutions. Within the G-77 itself, a rethinking produced quiet abandonment of "global negotiations" focused solely in the General Assembly and UNCTAD in 1983–4 in favor of a combined strategy of continuing broad discussions in those forums but dealing more with particular economic questions in the existing Bretton Woods and GATT institutions. The change became more apparent later in the decade, in statements issued by the NAM's (Nonaligned Movement) 1988 Foreign Ministers' meeting and 1989 Belgrade Summit.[20]

This sea change in economic sentiment transformed General Assembly debates on international economic questions. The economic differences between industrial and developing states did not disappear; if anything, the weak economic growth of the Middle East and Africa stood out more clearly. Nor were they suddenly irrelevant to governments' perspectives on how to regulate the international economy. However, the basis of debate shifted. No longer was it a question of whether to replace international markets and economic regimes with greater state regulation or planning; the question now was whether global markets should be organized along the lines of "embedded liberalism" or of "neoliberalism."

The Palestinian–Israeli conflict

Though the 1973 war had involved Arab states, initiative in the conflict was passing to the PLO even before Egypt upset the foundations of regional dynamics by deciding to make a separate peace with Israel in 1979. Whatever optimism that move generated soon faded as Palestinian Arabs and Israelis remained as far apart as ever on the future of the area. Their confrontation even spread to Lebanon as the ongoing Lebanese civil war allowed Palestinian militants to acquire *de facto* control of much of southern Lebanon. Though a UN force was stationed in Lebanon to help resolve the civil war, it lacked the mandate or the means to establish control over southern Lebanon. In June 1982, Israel took matters into its own hands by invading and attempting to root out Hezbollah and PLO camps, and considerable negotiating and pressuring was required to persuade the Israelis to withdraw.

The conflict took on an even more Palestinian versus Israeli complexion when Palestinians in East Jerusalem, the West Bank, and Gaza began the first *intifada* (uprising) in December 1987, destroying any notion that Israel could continue to ignore Palestinian claims to establish their own state there. The pressure on Israel intensified in November 1988 when the PLO declared Palestinian statehood and endorsed a "two-state solution" to the conflict and thereby Israel's right to exist. The PLO had long maintained that Palestinian self-determination should include independent statehood, but had not to that point acknowledged Israel's right to exist. While inspiring some US opening to the PLO, these steps elicited no response from Israel, opening it to condemnation in the Security Council and more extreme rhetoric in the General Assembly. The assembly majority at this point indicated its support for the PLO initiatives by upgrading the PLO to a status equivalent to that of a non-member state.[21]

After the Cold War

Leninism implodes

Pressing need to focus on internal reform led the Soviet leadership under Gorbachev to reduce its foreign policy commitments. This decision was reflected in several levels of policy change. For the General Assembly, the most dramatic was Gorbachev's insistence on the need for greater international co-operation, summed up in his 1987 assertion that "there are human tasks above those of the proletariat"[22] and more general call for "new thinking" in foreign affairs. The Soviet Union also began using the Security Council as a venue for working out co-operative arrangements to wind down various Third World conflicts in which it had become involved. This Soviet change of mind elicited some skepticism at first among Western governments, but captured the imagination of public opinion and Western governments, even the Reagan administration, came around.

Mutual readiness to wind down existing conflicts was most apparent in Central America, where stalemated local contenders were ready to accept both regional and UN conflict resolution efforts, and in Africa where the Soviets sought negotiated settlements to the conflicts in which they had been involved. The Gorbachev leadership also co-operated in efforts to help Iran and Iraq end their long-running war. Yet the most vivid sign of Soviet policy change was the decision to withdraw Soviet troops from Afghanistan. Even this required international co-operation because the Soviets were reluctant to see the regime they had been supporting for so long overthrown immediately by the US- and Pakistani-funded mujahedin. Institutionally, this greater use of the Security Council put the General Assembly in the shadow. However, member governments were happy to see the abatement of East–West conflict and seemed largely content with a return to the division of labor between UN bodies envisioned in 1945.

Another feature of the 1945 design was painfully visible in the dismantling of the Cold War division of Europe. Taking heart from, but going beyond, Gorbachev's insistence on the need for "new thinking," Eastern Europeans began demanding reform and even abolition of the communist regimes that had ruled their countries since the end of the Second World War. Throughout the unraveling process beginning on 25 October 1989, when the Soviets renounced the Brezhnev Doctrine of Soviet intervention to prevent the overthrow of communist governments in the area, and ending on 12 September 1990, when they agreed to reunification of Germany as a member of the NATO alliance rather than a neutral state, the United Nations stood on the sidelines.

Perceptions of rosy dawn

The Security Council, General Assembly, and other parts of the UN system fully shared the sense of euphoria that spread as the long East–West ideological and military competition came to an end. Resolving regional conflicts had lighted the burden felt by peoples around the world, and created hopes for better futures in the region. The impact of the dissolution of the Soviet bloc was far greater, summarized most eloquently by the pictures of Germans dancing on and next to the breached Berlin Wall on 9 November 1989. From Vancouver to Vladivostok, the popular mood could be summed up in the words used by William Wordsworth regarding the outbreak of the French Revolution: "bliss was it in that dawn to be alive."[23] In the General Assembly, the change was marked by adoption of a resolution co-sponsored by the US and the USSR on 15 November on co-operation in maintaining peace.[24] Governments and peoples alike saw momentous change and shared high expectations for peace, prosperity, and democracy in the coming century.

Confidence about the future, and the central place of the United Nations in it, was reinforced by events on the Arabian Peninsula after Iraq's invasion of Kuwait in August 1990. The well-armed Iraqis made short work of the tiny Kuwaiti forces, and occupied the whole country within 48 hours. Iraqi President Saddam Hussein did offer some explanations, accusing the Kuwaitis of drilling more than their share of a disputed oilfield and undercutting oil prices to Iraq's detriment, and also sought to inspire greater Arab support by promising to withdraw from Kuwait if Israel withdrew from the Occupied Territories. Local concern that Iraq could, if not stopped, expand its control over other parts of the Arabian Peninsula, combined with Western and Japanese concern about oil supplies raised widespread alarm.

Iraq's bold move galvanized those who saw the attack as naked aggression. Even two years earlier, an Iraqi invasion would have produced deadlock in the Security Council because of longstanding Soviet–Iraqi ties. Yet in August 1990, the Soviet leadership was prepared to accept a collective response. The Soviets tried to avert the coming counterattack against Iraq by negotiating some sort of settlement, but when Iraq failed to meet the 15 January 1991 deadline for withdrawal from Kuwait, they did not interfere with the ensuing war and joined in denying Iraq access to satellite intelligence. In the Kuwait War, the UN appeared to work as originally designed; the Security Council took charge, made clear who it regarded as the aggressor, insisted that the aggressor withdraw, and authorized "Member States cooperating with the Government of Kuwait" to use "all necessary means" to enforce Iraqi withdrawal.[25] As a victorious coalition returned to the Security Council to define the terms of peace with Iraq, governments and public around the world could easily conclude that collective security had worked and that the world was ready to return to the original design of the United Nations.

The general climate of optimism made it easier for the UN and its members to deal with what could have been a highly disruptive change when the Soviet Union itself dissolved in the fall of 1991. There were few examples of the peaceful decline of a great power to go on, yet the UN and its members handled the last bit of the post-Cold War transition well. Though scattered opposition was expressed, other governments rapidly agreed that the Russian Federation, the largest of the new states emerging from the Soviet collapse, should succeed to the Soviet position in the United Nations while the other post-Soviet republics applied for separate UN membership.[26]

The spread of market economics

The collapse of the Soviet Union reinforced the global shift to market economics by opening Eastern Europe, Russia, and Central Asia to market possibilities. The question now facing UN members was defining what form of market economics. The "neoliberals" (so-called to distinguish them from both early nineteenth-century advocates of markets and twentieth-century advocates of Keynesian-style "embedded liberalism") staked out their position first. With strong influence in both the US and British governments, and receptive groups elsewhere, neoliberals were in good position to advance their views within governments and multilateral economic institutions. They played the leading part in shaping the "Washington Consensus." It emphasized reliance on markets rather than planning, rapid privatization of state-owned economic enterprises, reliance on private investment raised domestically or on international financial markets, and reduction of state regulations regarding economic activity.[27]

However, the neoliberals faced serious intellectual and political challenges from others. In the industrial countries adherents of "rival capitalisms" – German social market or stakeholder capitalism, Japanese and East Asian government-organized capitalism – offered different visions of how to organize and regulate a market economy. In the developing countries, structuralist analyses of trade remained popular, though statism and de-linking were dropped in favor of markets and linking, and inspired complaints that Northern protectionism unfairly excludes developing countries from the full benefits of a global market.[28] In all countries advocates for workers and the poor condemned neoliberal policies for increasing inequality within and between countries.

These views were reflected in all of the UN discussions of development issues. Though abandoning efforts to develop a Human Freedom Index as too controversial, UNDP did reconceptualize its monitoring of national economic conditions to include quality of life indicators as well as economic data in its new Human Development Index. General Assembly discussion of development issues became occasions for arguing about what sort of market-based economy should be formed. Third World countries were aware that the end of the Cold War meant they could no longer play off one superpower against the other. This strengthened the pragmatic wing of the NAM and produced a more effective two-track economic diplomacy of engaging in each of the major economic institutions while pursuing broader discussions in the assembly, UN global conferences, and North–South summits.[29] At the same time, the end of the Cold War gave those Western governments so inclined more leeway to link aid and other concessions on economic issues to policy changes within developing states.

General Assembly resolutions on economic issues began to take new form in the late 1980s, specifying in separate sections policy directions for both developing and industrial countries. The former were urged to take particular steps to improve their own economic performance while the latter were urged to assist developing ones directly and through changes in the rules of the international economy.[30] In some ways, this was an extension of the debate over how to interpret the agreed phrase "common but differentiated responsibilities" that had emerged out of the 1992 UN Conference on Environment and Development in Rio de Janeiro. The general economic version was further enunciated in the 2001 "Monterrey Consensus" that governments of developing states have an obligation to pursue domestic reform to facilitate development while governments of industrial states have an obligation to provide meaningful assistance to the improved process of development.[31] Consensus that both North and South have particular tasks has not ended the South–North contention. The Group of 77 still wants more change in international economic rules than many of the industrial states are ready to support, and even the reduced goal of industrial states devoting 0.7 percent of their GNP to aid (rather than the 1 percent demanded in the mid-1970s) is met by few of them.[32]

Yet internal divisions among Third World governments and anti-globalization activists, as well as tensions between them as the activists emphasize human need more than sovereignty while the governments reverse those priorities, have inhibited development of a common alternative to the "Washington Consensus." Differences in economic performance, and hence economic concerns, among developing countries grew even wider. Though intense at the time, the "Asian crisis" of 1997–8 proved to be a short interruption in a long period of rapid growth in that region. Somewhat higher oil prices and earnings on foreign investment could not hide the fact that most Middle-Eastern economies were not diversifying away from dependence on oil. Almost every African country, but particularly those racked by civil war or ethnic conflict, was poorer in 2000 than it had been in 1980.

Individual developing countries' understandings of their more specific economic interests were also becoming more divergent as active manufacturing sectors formed in some: strong information technology sectors developed in a few (most notably India), and raw materials or agricultural commodities remained the main exports of others. As economic discussions moved from statements of abstract principle to the specifics of particular types of transactions or regulations covering particular sectors, it was more and more difficult to maintain a united Group of 77. Yet the North was no more united, with the Japanese and Europeans far more receptive to notions of government regulation than either of the Bush administrations in the US, and industrial states were also divided by specific interests arising out of the shape of their national economies.

Democratic rule

The waning of the Cold War followed and reinforced the spread of democratic rule that began in Latin America in the early 1980s and had spread to East Asia in the mid-1980s. Forcible suppression of the Chinese democracy movement in Tienamin Square in 1989 checked, but did not reverse, the trend. Eastern Europe and the former Soviet republics were relative latecomers to the transition, which they reinforced by example and by disproving the claims of some in the West that Leninist governments would be able to surmount the popular pressures that had overwhelmed many right-wing dictatorships.[33]

This spreading of democracy led, for the first time, to serious discussion of the proposition that UN member states should be expected not only to respect human rights but also to organize their internal politics on the model of multiparty democracy with periodic free elections. The UN Charter had always specified that member states must be "peace loving." Yet that term had never been defined, and the fact that a large portion of the UN's membership has been involved in one or more armed conflicts since 1945 suggests "peace loving" does not mean pacifist. The Charter was silent on the internal organization of states. The norms enunciated by the General Assembly emphasized member state sovereignty, self-determination of peoples, and nonintervention in the internal affairs of other states much more than promotion of human rights. Even the human rights portions of the Charter were understood to permit each state to choose its own form of government.

The question of whether the United Nations should require member states to adopt democratic forms of governance arose in the wake of developments in Europe. In November 1990 the members of the Organization for Security and Co-operation in Europe declared in their Charter of Paris that "we intend to build, consolidate, and strengthen democracy as the only system of government of our nations."[36] Proposals that the General Assembly endorse democratic rule in general terms, the more specific notion that peoples should be able to choose their political leaders through periodic, free, and fair elections, or even the very ambitious idea that peoples and individuals have a right to democratic governance were very controversial. Third World governments worried that such norms would provide another justification for external meddling in their countries' affairs. However, many of them were caught in a political vise because their own peoples, aware of and inspired by the Eastern European examples, were demanding political change at home. The assembly has resolved this dilemma by adopting contradictory resolutions: some endorsing democratic rule in broad terms, and others emphasizing the need to respect each state's sovereignty and each people's right to make its own decisions. Debates on human rights show equally contradictory trends; some general endorsements but also considerable maneuvering to secure or avert condemnation of a particular government's actions.

Optimism recedes

The euphoria of 1989 began to recede owing to events on the same continent that had given rise to it. As Yugoslavia broke into its component republics in 1990–1, it became more widely understood that the internal boundaries between republics becoming the new international borders did not always follow the ethnic divisions among the Yugoslav population. With the unifying ideology of "Titoism" (a variant of reform Leninism) gone, ethnonationalist extremists, particularly in Serbia, soon set off a series of devastating conflicts. They would have been "internal conflicts" had the international community chosen to reject dismemberment of Yugoslavia, and as such might not have triggered demands for UN involvement. However, the Western European decision to accept the various republics as independent states, triggered by German recognition of Croatia in 1992, made them "international conflicts." The war in the Balkans was quickly followed by the initiation or the wider publicizing of other interethnic wars. By mid-1993, public discussions of security featured lengthy discourses on the intractability of ethnic conflict, based as it was on supposedly primordial and persistent hatreds. The slow international and UN response to the conflicts in former Yugoslavia, and the failure to do anything about the genocide in Rwanda, inspired severe criticisms and great doubts about both the effectiveness of the Security Council and the readiness of major member states to take effective action.

The Palestinian–Israeli conflict

Optimism was also eroded by renewed stalemate in the Israeli–Palestinian conflict after some period of progress towards a negotiated solution through the Oslo peace process. Rejectionists on both sides intensified the conflict, with the Israelis saddled with most of the blame around the world for their lengthy refusal to remove Jewish settlements from West Bank areas outside the 1967 borders and their use of harsh measures to deal with ongoing attacks by Palestinian and other Arab extremists. Faced with fragmentation on other issues, support for the Palestinian right of self-determination is now an important source of NAM unity. Increased concern about terrorism, and all the talk about a broad confrontation between "Islam" and "the West," has aided the Palestinians by providing more opportunities for insisting that the main cause of Middle East instability is not political Islamicist movements, but continuing US support for Israel. Israel continues to be perceived as a colonial-era creation, and the 1948 displacement of Palestinians is now being described as an "ethnic cleansing" for which Israel must be called to account in some way.[37] Whether the possibilities of settlement that appeared to open up after Yasir Arafat's death in November 2004 will be grasped on both sides remains to be seen.

Facing the challenge of terrorist groups

Encouraged by the second Bush administration, insular Americans regard the September 11 attacks on the World Trade Center and the Pentagon as the start of a new era. However, people in other countries had known for many years that transnationally operating terrorist groups posed a significant threat to public safety. Both the Security Council and the General Assembly had been addressing the issue of international terrorism for more than two decades, at an accelerating pace in the 1990s as a wider array of transnational terrorist groups became visible. There was broad consensus that such groups' ability to exploit the transportation, communications, and money-transfer possibilities of globalization did pose a qualitatively new threat, but considerable disagreement about how to deal with that threat.

Dealing with the threat has been complicated by the looseness of the language used in the debates. Violent political movements in many parts of the world have resorted to "terrorist tactics" like taking hostages, hijacking commercial aircraft, blowing up electrical power stations, and setting off bombs in public places like subway lines. During the Cold War the maxim "one person's terrorist is another's freedom fighter" summed up much of the reaction to the problem. Only with the end of the Cold War were governments prepared to step back and ask whether nonstate groups should be permitted to use whatever violent tactics they chose, or whether, like the armed forces of states,[34] they should be expected to show restraint in their choice of targets for attack. By the late 1990s, though with considerable misgiving among Arab states seeking to ensure that the Palestinians were not defined as terrorists, the General Assembly had endorsed the idea that certain tactics should be regarded as illegitimate no matter what the cause for which a group is fighting. At the same time, it favored a law enforcement rather than a military approach to the problem, urging member governments to ratify and apply the 12 multilateral conventions on terrorist acts.

The September 2001 attacks revealed a new dimension to the problem. Unlike the Palestinians, or the Tamil "Tigers" fighting in Sri Lanka, the authors of those attacks, a network known under the collective name Al Qaeda ("The Base") had more diffuse goals. Some were political; Al Qaeda insisted that it was supporting the Palestinian cause by attacking Israel's strongest supporter, and also urged the establishment of Islamicist governments in predominantly Muslim countries. Other goals were as much cultural as political, reflecting a generalized rejection of secular modernity and Western influence on other parts of the world.

Immediately after the September 2001 attacks, nearly every government in the world agreed that Al Qaeda and other transnational terrorist groups posed a common danger. Thus, after the Taliban government of Afghanistan refused to order closure of Al Qaeda camps in that country and turn over Osama bin Laden and other Al Qaeda leaders to the US for trial, the Security Council accepted the US government claim that its invasion of Afghanistan was an act of self-defense. The same co-operative mood led to greater co-ordination among national law-enforcement agencies in their efforts to hobble terrorist groups by shutting down their money laundering, identifying and arresting individual members when they could be charged with crimes, and developing warnings of when terrorist activity might be occurring.

The co-operative mood was shattered in 2002–3 when the Bush administration sought to justify its invasion of Iraq by claiming, among other duplicitous arguments, that the government of Saddam Hussein had been co-operating with terrorist groups. Failing in its efforts to persuade the Security Council to endorse an invasion of Iraq, the Bush administration pressed forward anyway. Criticism from other governments was intense, and massive popular anti-war demonstrations were held around the world. The military campaign was over quickly, so quickly that any thoughts of convening an emergency session of the General Assembly dissipated. However, the mood in the assembly remained sour as the war was seen as simply the most flamboyant example of a more general US disregard for the opinions of the rest of the world, affecting debates on economic, environmental, and human rights issues as well as on security questions.

Change and the assembly

Throughout its history the United Nations, including the General Assembly, has been shaped by the international context and the choices of its member states. Delegates in the General Assembly, particularly those from smaller states whose governments leave them considerable discretion, develop an *esprit de corps* that makes them more sensitive to the "international opinion" expressed by their peers than national political leaders or their officials bureaucrats at home.[35] Yet their ability to steer changes in the international context or affect the choices of major governments at a particular moment is quite limited. Over time, however, debates in the General Assembly do have a potential for affecting governments' choices, and thereby contributing to the evolution of the international context.

Neither majorities nor minorities have used the assembly particularly well. They have seldom used it for real deliberation; projecting a particular view of the world, protecting their friends (easier for the majority), and harassing their rivals has absorbed most of their energy. Political bodies always elicit those sorts of behaviors; the problem with the assembly is how far they have come to overshadow the deliberative functions. Today the assembly is caught between two inimical forces. The first is a US government strongly influenced by long-time critics of the UN who would be happiest if it disappeared. The second is a Third World majority organized into large caucuses that can maintain cohesion among states with very different interests and identities only through a politics of summing demands together, which makes them appear to be "engines of group-think, given to lowest common denominator outcomes"[38] unlikely to be sources of new ideas for establishing more humane governance around the world.

Understanding the extent and limits of the influence that a well-used assembly could exert requires examining how the General Assembly operates – the subject of Chapter 3 – and the character of its relationships with other UN bodies and with member governments – the subject of Chapter 4.

Notes

1 For example Marie-Claude Smouts, "The General Assembly: grandeur and deca-dence," in Paul Taylor and A.J.R. Groom (eds) *The United Nations at the Millennium* (London: 2000), 21–60.

2 David Mitrany, *A Working Peace System* (London: 1943).

3 Discussions at the Inter-American Conference on the Problems of Peace and War, Mexico City, 21 February–8 March 1945.

4 Speech to the South African Parliament, Cape Town, 4 Feb 1960, *New York Times* 4 Feb 1960, p.1.

5 Philip Bobbett, *The Shield of Achilles* (New York: 2002) provides a particularly cogent discussion of the change and its implications.

6 GA Resolution 1514 (XV) of 14 December 1960.

7 See Adam M. Garfinkle, "On the origin, meaning, use, and abuse of a phrase," *Middle Eastern Studies* 27(4): 539–50 (October 1991).

8 Albert Hourani, *A History of the Arab Peoples* (Cambridge, MA: 1991), 323.

9 See Arthur Lall, *The United Nations and the Middle East Crisis, 1967* (rev. edn, New York: 1970), 175.

10 John Ruggie, "International regimes, transactions, and change," *International Organization* 36(2): 379–415 (spring 1982), provides one of the best short exposi-tions of embedded liberalism.

11 Some observers, including Hernane Tavares da Sa, *The Play within the Play: The Inside Story of the UN* (New York: 1966), 67–8, believed that the Soviets consciously undermined Beijing's chances.

12 GA Resolution 1897 (XVIII) of 11 November 1963.

13 Commonplace phrase, used as a section title in *Foreign Policy*, No. 14, Spring 1974, pp. 56–90.

14 Good summaries of the NIEO program include Craig N. Murphy, "What the Third World wants," *International Studies Quarterly* 27(1): 55–76 (1983).

15 GA Resolutions 3201 (S-VI) of 1 May 1974; vote in A/S-VI/PV. 2229 (1 May 1974) and 3281 (XXIX) of 12 December 1974, vote in A/29/PV.2319 (12 December 1974).

16 Resolution 3379 (XXX) of 10 November 1975. Vote in UN Doc A/30/PV. (10 November 1975).

17 Andrei Amalrik, *Will the Soviet Union Survive until 1984?* (New York: 1970); Western estimates recalled in Daniel Patrick Moynihan, *Pandaemonium* (Oxford: 1993), 34–44.

18 Elizabeth Kridl Valkenier, *The Soviet Union and the Third World: An Economic Bind* (New York: 1983).
19 Explained cogently by Padma Desai, "The Soviet Union and the Third World," in Jagdish N. Bhagwati and John Gerard Ruggie (eds) *Power, Passions, and Purpose* (Cambridge, MA: 1984), 261–85.
20 Sally Morphet, "States groups at the United Nations and the growth of member states at the United Nations," in Paul Taylor and A.J.R. Groom (eds), *The United Nations at the Millennium: The Principal Organs* (London and New York: 2000), 253.
21 Resolution 43/177 of 15 December 1988.
22 "The reality and guarantees of a secure world," *Pravda*, 17 September 1987, pp. 1–2.
23 "French Revolution, as it appeared to enthusiasts at its commencement," *The Complete Poetical Works of Wordsworth* (Boston: Houghton-Mifflin, 1982), 340.
24 Resolution 44/21 "Enhancing international peace, security, and international co-operation in all of its aspects in accordance with the Charter of the United Nations."
25 SC Resolution 678 of 29 November 1990.
26 Akmaral Arystanbekova, "Kazakhstan: ten years in the United Nations," *International Affairs* (Moscow) 48(4): 150–6 (2002), says some Africans proposed substituting a Third World state.
27 Summarized in John Williamson, *The Progress of Policy Reform in Latin America* (Washington: Institute for International Economics, 1990).
28 South Centre, *The Challenge to the South* (Oxford: 1990).
29 As some Third World commentators had been urging for some years. See, e.g., T.N. Srinivasan, "Why developing countries should participate in the GATT system," *World Economy* 5(1) pp. 85–104 (March 1982).
30 For instance, GA Resolution 43/27 on "Mid-term review and appraisal of the United Nations Programme of Action for African Recovery and Development 1986–1990" of 18 November 1988 and GA Resolution 46/151 on "Final review and appraisal" of 18 December 1991.
31 UN Doc. A/CONF.198/3, 22 March 2002 [Monterrey Consensus].
32 An insightful overview is provided in Jacques Fomerand, "The politics of norm-setting in the United Nations: the case of sustainable human development," in Dennis Dijkzeul and Yves Beigbeder (eds), *Rethinking International Organizations: Pathologies and Promise* (New York and Oxford: 203), 77–101.
33 Most famously Jeanne Kirkpatrick, *Dictatorships and Double Standards* (New York: 1982), a neoconservative argument for the need to reintensify ideological competition.
34 Charter of Paris, 21 November 1990.
35 See Illan Pappe, "The Geneva bubble," *London Review of Books*, 8 January 2004, 17–18. Pappe himself suggests a truth and reconciliation commission to bring the whole history out and ensure official Israeli acknowledgment of the wrong. Emergence of the usage also indicates intensification of the de-legitimization of boundaries different than existed in 1967 or even under the 1947 partition plan by adding "ethnic cleansing" to the list of Israeli violations of international law.
36 As the Secretary-General's High Level Panel on Threats, Challenges, and Change notes in *A More Secure World; Our Common Responsibility*, par. 164.
37 See, for example, R. Peck, "Socialization of permanent representatives in the United Nations," *International Organization* 33(3): 365–390 (1979).
38 The phrase comes from Paul Heinbecker, recently retired Canadian ambassador to the UN, in "Washington's exceptionalism and the United Nations," *Global Governance* 10(3): 278 (2004).

3 The General Assembly process

Political institutions provide sites where participants try to advance their political goals by means consistent with the norms of behavior established in the institution's written and unwritten procedural rules. Because no one institution facilitates attainment of every possible political goal, participants must select what they will pursue where. The General Assembly is a deliberative body most adapted to elaboration of general norms and standards for member state conduct, but it can also provide an arena where parties to a conflict can appeal to a wider audience. Like other deliberative bodies, the assembly has fairly elaborate rules, a few specified in the UN Charter, others contained in successive versions of the Rules of Procedure,[1] and many established by practice.

Regular assembly sessions run from the third Tuesday in September through the third week in December, with some additional meetings in the spring. Foreign ministers and heads of government frequently attend the early meetings devoted to the annual General Debate, sometimes launching proposals (such as Soviet Premier Khrushchev's 1960 idea of replacing the Secretary-General with a three-person committee) and at other times articulating their view of the world situation (such as US President George H.W. Bush's description of the emerging "new world order" in 1991). The UN Secretary-General now summarizes his annual Report on the Work of the Organization early in the session; the full report is the first substantive document delegates receive.[2]

The participants

Delegates

Most of the over 1,000 participants in a General Assembly session are delegates appointed by the government of each member state. The UN Charter and General Assembly rules only specify their number; Charter Article 9(2) limits each member to "not more than five representatives" while assembly rule 25 permits adding up to five alternate representatives and as many experts and advisers as desired. In 2004, delegations ranged in size from three (Turkmenistan) to 121 (Germany).[3] Assembly insiders agree that a new delegate needs about a year to learn all the skills of multilateral diplomacy. Most governments therefore keep the key members of their UN missions and assembly delegations in place for at least four years and typically select their senior delegates from among officials with prior experience in UN bodies. However, the larger delegations also include persons who serve for one session only or attend only part of the session.

Delegates work for the government that sends them, and it instructs them about goals to seek, positions to take, and tactics to pursue. However, the range of detail in these instructions is vast, as Edvard Hambro described nicely in 1972:

> Rumor has it that a permanent representative ... cabled home for instructions during an important crisis and was told in no uncertain terms that he was sent to New York to take care of that part of the policy of his country, and that his asking for instructions was quite uncalled for.
>
> Another delegate ... not only gets detailed instructions about every vote, but has all speeches sent verbatim from his capital with instructions of when to speak sincerely and when to inject an ironic inflection.[4]

Interaction among delegates is sufficiently extensive that everyone quickly discerns who has detailed instructions and who has more general ones. Soviet bloc delegates were very closely instructed, and their activity monitored by their own country's intelligence agency. Western delegates receive extensive instructions reflecting both the bureaucratic politics within the government and pressures by the legislature, interest groups, or public opinion. Delegates from African and Pacific Island states generally have the least detailed instructions. Yet all governments provide closer guidance when an issue is important to major foreign policy goals or involves significant monetary commitments. On issues regarded as less important, governments provide broad guidelines such as "vote with the regional group," "you can abstain if _____ votes no, otherwise vote in favor," or "avoid being left in an isolated position," and usually leave procedural choices to their delegates.

The dynamics of multilateral diplomacy, reinforced over the decades by improvements in telecommunications, create a two-way relation between governments and their delegates. Reduced telecommunications costs[5] have enabled all delegations, not just those from wealthy governments, to contact their home governments as needed. Governments learn what is happening in the assembly from their delegates, who also explain the full meaning of proposed resolutions, suggest tactical possibilities, or indicate when taking up a question through bilateral channels would helpfully reinforce diplomatic efforts in New York. In turn, governments can update instructions daily or even more frequently. General Assembly rules and practices accommodate securing additional instructions as needed. Committee plans of work and meeting schedules published in the *Journal of the United Nations* indicate what issues will be discussed when. Informal consultations mean delegates know the general terms, and often the exact language, of draft resolutions before they are formally submitted. Assembly rules 78 and 120 require submitting proposed resolutions and amendments in writing 24 hours prior to voting, and this rule is seldom waived. Delegates needing further instructions at voting time can request a further delay, and such requests are usually granted because all delegates know that they may need to ask for a delay on some other occasion.

Delegations also need to ensure that their own members are not working at cross-purposes. Sufficiently large delegations assign different members to particular committees or issues; all draw on the staff of their country's Permanent Mission to the UN for assistance in keeping track of discussions. Wealthy countries can support large missions; the smallest and poorest generally economize by accrediting some staff to both their embassy to the US and their UN Mission, shifting them between Washington and New York as needed. Co-ordination occurs in delegation meetings, which vary in frequency and formality. Most delegations find it necessary to meet at least once a week, usually in the morning before the plenary and main committees convene.

Regional and other caucusing groups

Individual members of national legislatures are grouped into clusters of the politically like-minded through political parties. Delegates to the General Assembly operate in a very different context. Unlike national legislators, they are not trustees chosen by the voters to promote some publicly advocated set of policies in a centralized and hierarchical political system. Rather, they are appointees of governments unwilling to cede much authority to the assembly (or any other part of the UN system). However, delegates need others' support to get their proposals adopted, and quickly develop a sense of who else is more or less like-minded on various issues. Linkages among like-minded delegations appeared very early in the League of Nations Assembly, where several identifiable clusters of generally like-minded governments – the Latin American states, the British Commonwealth, the "Little Entente" of Czechoslovakia, Romania, and Yugoslavia, and a more amorphous Balkan group – soon emerged.[6]

Despite this League experience, neither the UN Charter nor the initial assembly rules of procedure mentioned caucusing groups of any sort. However, groups did begin to emerge in 1945–6 when the assembly faced the task of choosing member states to fill the nonpermanent seats on the Security Council. Because the shape of postwar political alignments among states was not yet clear, the assembly adopted a loosely geographic system of selection that divided member states into five groups: British Commonwealth (five states), Asia and the Mideast (eight), Latin America (twenty), Eastern Europe (five), and Western Europe (six). The same groupings, plus a separate category of "permanent members of the Security Council" established to respect the under-standing that all five would be included among the Assembly vice presidents and on other bodies, were used in other assembly elections.

Two factors limited the political significance acquired by most of these electoral clusters during the assembly's first decade. First, there was some uncertainty about which states belonged to which group, particularly as the newly independent British colonies began gravitating towards their geographical region rather than the Commonwealth. Second, the assembly made so little use of informal negotiations and consensus-seeking as the Cold War set in that the regional groups did not acquire a caucusing role. The uncertainty was intensified as UN membership rose from 60 states in 1954 to 100 in 1960. The influx enlarged the assembly significantly and trans-formed what had been a predominantly European and Latin American body into a majority African and Asian one, as can be seen in Table 3.1. When new electoral clusters were formally defined in 1962–3 the former British colonies joined the "Afro-Asian" cluster for elections while the white-settled "Old Dominions" of Australia, Canada, New Zealand, and South Africa were joined with the Western Europeans to form a new Western European and Other (WEO) Group.[7] Two further transformations of groups occurred as UN membership continued to rise. By 1975 Asian members rivaled Africans in number, and lobbied successfully for splitting the Afro-Asian group in two. After 1991 the former Soviet republics had to select a group, with the Baltic states, Armenia, Azerbaijan, and Georgia joining the Eastern European group while the Central Asian republics gravitated to the Asian group.[8]

Developments after 1962 spurred the evolution of most of the regional electoral clusters groups into caucusing groups. The Latin Americans consciously operated as a group from the start, hoping to translate their numbers into more influence in the UN than they had acquired in the more Europe-centered League of Nations.[9] Adding Yugoslavia to the Afro-Asian group in 1955 had two results. First, it reinforced the group's position as the nucleus of the emerging Nonaligned Movement (NAM), which was already unhappy about the East–West stalemate over admission of additional members to the UN and would explicitly organize as a collective effort to avoid Cold War alignments in 1961.[10] Second, with the dissident Yugoslavia

Table 3.1 Regional composition of the General Assembly.

	Total	African	Asian [a]	Latin American	Eastern European	Western
1945	51	3	9	20	6	13
1946	55	3	11	20	6	15
1947	57	3	13	20	6	15
1948	58	3	14	20	6	15
1949	59	3	14	20	6	16
1950	60	3	15	20	6	16
1951	60	3	15	20	6	16
1952	60	3	15	20	6	16
1953	60	3	15	20	6	16
1954	60	3	15	20	6	16
1955	76	4	20	20	10[b]	22
1956	80	7	21	20	10	22
1957	82	8	22	20	10	22
1958	82	9	21[c]	20	10	22
1959	82	9	21	20	10	22
1960	99	26	22	20	10	22
1961	104	28	24[d]	20	10	22
1962	110	32	24	22[e]	10	22
1963	113	34	25	22	10	22
1964	115	36[f]	25	22	10	22
1965	117	37	26[g]	22	10	22
1966	122	39	27[h]	24	10	22

Continued on page 46

(Table 3.1 continued)

	Total	African	Asian [a]	Latin American	Eastern European	Western
1967	123	39	28	24	10	22
1968	126	42	28	24	10	22
1969	126	42	28	24	10	22
1970	127	42	29	24	10	22
1971	132	42	34	24	10	22
1972	132	42	34	24	10	22
1973	135	42	34	25	11	23
1974	138	43	35	26	11	23
1975	144	47	36	27	11	23
1976	147	49	37	27	11	23
1977	149	50	38	27	11	23
1978	151	50	39	28	11	23
1979	152	50	39	29	11	23
1980	154	51	39	30	11	23
1981	157	51	40	32	11	23
1982	157	51	40	32	11	23
1983	158	51	40	33	11	23
1984	159	51	41	33	11	23
1985	159	51	41	33	11	23
1986	159	51	41	33	11	23
1987	159	51	41	33	11	23
1988	159	51	41	33	11	23

Continued on page 47

Table 3.1 continued

	Total	African	Asian [a]	Latin American	Eastern European	Western
1988	159	51	41	33	11	23
1989	159	51	41	33	11	23
1990	159	52	40[i]	33	10[j]	24
1991	166	52	44	33	19	25
1992	179	52	50	33	19[k]	25
1993	184	53	50	33	20[l]	26
1994	185	53	50	33	20	26
1995	185	53	50	33	20	26
1996	185	53	50	33	20	26
1997	185	53	50	33	20	26
1998	185	53	50	33	20	26
1999	188	53	53	33	20	26
2000	189	53	54	33	21[m]	26
2001	189	53	54	33	21	26
2002	191	53	55	33	21	27
2003	191	53	55	33	21	27

Source: M.J. Peterson, *The General Assembly in World Politics* (London: 1986), 292–3; Sally Morphet, "States groups at the United Nations," in Paul Taylor and A.J.R. Groom (eds), *The United Nations at the Millennium: The Principal Organs* (London: 2000), Table 8, 262–5; calculations based on UN website list of members.

Notes
a   Israel is included in the Asian count, though excluded from the group. It has been treated as a member of the Western European and Other group on the few occasions when it has been elected to a UN Committee
b   Yugoslavia was included in the Afro-Asian group for elections in 1955–70
c   Egypt and Syria merged to form the United Arab Republic
d   Syria withdrew from the UAR and resumed its separate membership
e   Cuba was excluded from group caucuses
f   Tanganyika (member since 1961 and Zanzibar (member since 1963) merged to form Tanzania

g   Indonesia withdrew from membership
h   Indonesia returned to membership
i   North and South Yemen merged
j   East Germany merged with West Germany
k   The SC and GA determined that Yugoslavia's membership had ended with dissolution of the
    Socialist Federated Republic of Yugoslavia in 1991–2
l   The Czech Republic and Slovakia admitted after agreed dissolution of Czechoslovakia
m   Federal Republic of Yugoslavia (Serbia and Montenegro since 2003) admitted (academic
    observers drop the SFRY from and add the FRY to the Eastern European Group in 1993 and
    2000 respectively, but UN compilations leave it in the total of member states during the
    interval between memberships)

gone, the Eastern European group remained a highly cohesive caucus cotermi-
nous with the USSR and its European allies. In contrast, the WEO included
both US allies and the European neutrals, and did not develop into a cohesive
caucus.

The impetus for caucusing became stronger in the 1960s for two reasons.
First, the overlap between regional groups and substantive like-mindedness in
economic affairs was accentuated in 1964 when the assembly organized
UNCTAD on the basis of four groups (A: Afro-Asian, B: Western industrial,
C: Latin American, and D: planned economy). Groups A and C quickly
merged into the Group of 77, a wider grouping than the NAM because it
included Latin American states, which focused on economic issues.[11] By
directing its demands for development assistance and changes in governance
of the international economy to Group B, the Group of 77 promoted a greater
degree of co-ordination among the leading Western industrial states. Second,
increasing UN membership and lengthening assembly agendas meant that
delegates could not keep up with the workload unless they supplemented the
formal meetings with informal consultations. Regional groups became not
only places where inexperienced delegates from new governments could get
advice from older hands, but also key structures in the increasing number of
informal consultations.

Public demonstration of how regional group-based informal consultations
could structure assembly proceedings came during the "voteless 19th session"
held while the superpowers argued out the question of whether peacekeeping
expenses are or are not part of the regular UN budget. The assembly met, but
discussed and adopted only those resolutions that could be accepted without a
vote.[12] The regional groups' significance was acknowledged in 1971 when the
Journal of the United Nations began listing their chairmen, a useful service
since most regional and other caucusing groups change leadership more than
once a year.

Caucuses also need to co-ordinate activities. By 1968 the regional groups
doubling as political caucuses had developed the two-tier structure of co-
ordination[13] still used today. Heads of delegation meet to select candidates for

assembly elections or to discuss the most important issues; the delegates covering particular committees or issues meet to co-ordinate tactics and work out proposals on matters within their purview.

Each regional group has a distinctive dynamic shaped by its history and the dynamics among subregional clusters of member states. Until 1989 the Eastern European group was acknowledged to be the most cohesive, the closest assembly analog to a national political party. It was relatively small, united by a common ideology, and had a clear leader willing and able to discipline its followers. Members, particularly Yugoslavia, which returned to the group for electoral purposes after 1970, sometimes advanced distinctive positions on certain issues, but the Eastern Europe group always scored highest in quantitative measures of voting blocs in the assembly.[14]

Economic issues provided a basis for strong cohesion within and between the African, Asian, and Latin American groups in the 1960s and 1970s. Pressing for rapid decolonization, supporting the Palestinians, and (until 1994) condemning South African apartheid provided additional rallying points. However, all three groups became less cohesive in the 1980s and 1990s as countries experienced different degrees of economic success and become more attuned to the opportunities and constraints of operating in a globalizing market.

The WEO has always been the least cohesive of the regional groups. The old differences between NATO members and European neutrals are no longer relevant, but differences between the US (with British support on many political issues) and the Western Europeans (especially France) have widened. The European Community/European Union and the Scandinavian clusters have been the most coherent subregional groupings in the WEO. On development questions, the main division has been between the USA, Germany, Britain, and Japan on one side and the more Third World-sympathetic France, Netherlands, and Scandinavians on the other.

Regional groups do not exhaust the caucusing within the assembly. The Nonaligned, which operates both within and outside the UN, and the Group of 77, which operates within, are the largest and most visible caucuses. The Nonaligned has triennial summits; the Group of 77 sometimes also holds whole-group meetings during assembly sessions. However, most interregional meetings occur among smaller groups of delegations designated by their respective groups to see if they can agree on some common position. In the 1970s and 1980s, the Group of 77 and the Nonaligned were effectively led by a small group of delegates including the Algerians, Cubans, Egyptians, and Pakistanis, adroit at limiting the impact of in-group ideological disagreements by focusing on the rallying points. More recently, the Nonaligned and Group of 77 have become weaker as the African, Asian, and Latin American groups comprising them have become more clearly divided into "ideological" and "pragmatic" camps,[15] but a new leadership including South Africa and Malaysia is working to hold the group together.[16] Less publicly visible, but weighty within the assembly, is the "Geneva Group" of industrial states. Each pays more than 1 percent of UN assessments, some considerably more, and they co-ordinate positions on budget and spending questions.

Other caucuses have not, however, eroded the roles of the regional groups or the Third World interregional clusters of Nonaligned and G-77. Many observers believe, however, that these groups inhibit needed change in the assembly's practices because they have developed such strong inertia. While acknowledging the current lack of any other basis for organizing stable caucuses, the High Level Panel on Threats, Challenges, and Change did propose altering the dynamics by reorganizing the assembly into four major regional groups: Africa (53 states), Asia and Pacific (56 states), Europe (47 states), and Americas (35 states).[17] "Europe" would confirm the end of the East–West divide and nest even an enlarged EU within, "Asia and the Pacific" and "Americas" would continue an existing regional group and create a new one with members spanning the South–North divide.

Officers of the General Assembly and the main committees

Even a small deliberative body needs a presiding member to prepare the daily agenda, encourage the body to stay focused on the matter at hand, and summarize the group's conclusions. A large deliberative body divided into committees also needs a co-ordinating group to parcel out the work among committees, monitor their progress, and prompt them to stay on schedule. The UN Charter says little about the internal organization of the General Assembly: Article 21 specifies that "it shall elect its president for each session" and Article 22 permits it to "establish such subsidiary organs as it deems necessary for the performance of its functions." Assembly rules and practices are the primary sources of guidance on officer authority and internal organization.

Assembly and main committee officers serve for one year. The presidency and committee offices rotate among the regional groups; as noted below, the vice presidencies are divided among them. The regions typically choose a different country for the regional "slots" while the five permanent members of the Security Council are always included among the vice presidents. Though chosen from among the national delegates, the assembly president, the main committee chairs, and the main committee rapporteurs always handed the task of representing their country to a fellow delegate for the duration of the session and served as individuals. The written rules specify that states are elected as assembly vice presidents and main committee vice chairs, and for many years any member of that state's delegation could preside when the president or chair was absent. As vice presidents and vice chairs acquired

Table 3.2 Presidents of the General Assembly.

Session/Year	President
1/1946	Paul-Henri Spaak, Belgium
2/1947	Oswaldo Aranha, Brazil
3/1948	Jose Arce, Argentina
4/1949	H.V. Evatt, Australia
5/1950	Carlos P. Romulo, Philippines
6/1951	Nasrollah Entezam, Iran
7/1952	Luis Padilla Nervo, Mexico
8/1953	Lester B. Pearson, Canada
9/1954	Vijaya Lakshmi Pandit, India
10/1955	Jose Maza, Chile
11/1956	Prince Wan Waithayakon, Thailand
12/1957	Sir Leslie Munro, New Zealand
13/1958	Charles Malik, Lebanon
14/1959	Victor Andres Belaunde, Peru
15/1960	Frederick H. Boland, Ireland
16/1961	Mongi Slim, Tunisia
17/1962	Sir Muhammed Zarfulla Khan, Pakistan
18/1963	Carlos Sosa Rodriguez, Venezuela
19/1964	Alex Quaison-Sackey, Ghana
20/1965	Amintore Fanfani, Italy
21/1966	Abdul Rahman Pazhwak, Afghanistan
22/1967	Corneliu Manescu, Romania
23/1968	Emilio Arenales Catalan, Guatemala
24/1969	Angie E. Brooks, Liberia
25/1970	Edvard Hambro, Norway
26/1971	Adam Malik, Indonesia
27/1972	Stanislaw Trepczynski, Poland
28/1973	Leopoldo Benites, Ecuador
29/1974	Abdelaziz Bouteflika, Algeria
30/1975	Gaston Thorn, Luxembourg
31/1976	Hamilton Shirley Amerasinghe, Sri Lanka
32/1977	Lazar Mojsov, Yugoslavia
33/1978	Indalecio Lievano, Colombia
34/1979	Salim A. Salim, Tanzania
35/1980	Ruder von Wechman, West Germany
36/1981	Ismat T. Kittani, Iraq
37/1982	Imre Hollai, Hungary
38/1983	Jorge Illueca, Panama

Continued on page 52

Table 3.2 continued

Session/Year	President
39/1984	Paul J.F. Lusaka, Zambia
40/1985	Jaime de Pinies, Spain
41/1986	Humayun Rasheed Choudhury, Bangladesh
42/1987	Peter Florin, East Germany
43/1988	Dante Caputo, Argentina
44/1989	Joseph Nanven Garba, Nigeria
45/1990	Guido de Marco, Malta
46/1991	Sami S. Shihabi, Saudi Arabia
47/1992	Stoyan Ganev, Bulgaria
48/1993	Samuel R. Insanally, Guyana
49/1994	Amara Essay, Cote d'Ivoire
50/1995	Diogo Fritas do Amaral, Portugal
51/1996	Razali Ismail, Malaysia
52/1997	Hennadiy Udovenko, Ukraine
53/1998	Didier Opertti, Uruguay
54/1999	Theo-Ben Gurirab, Namibia
55/2000	Harri Holkeri, Finland
56/2001	Han Seung-soo, South Korea
57/2002	Jan Kavan, Czech Republic
58/2003	Julian Robert Hunte, Saint Lucia
59/2004	Jean Ping, Gabon
60/2005	Jan Eliasson, Sweden

Source: UN Department of Public Information at *www.un.org/*

greater leadership roles in the informal discussions, these offices also settled on a particular senior member of the delegation who leaves national representation tasks to others.

While the assembly has always had one president, the numbers of vice presidents and committee chairs have varied. At the first session there were seven vice presidents and six main committee chairs, forming with the president a General Committee of 14 members. The number of main committee chairs increased to seven in 1947, and returned to six in 1993. The number of vice presidents was increased three times to permit greater representation for the regional groupings, ending with 21 in 1978. Unwritten understandings about selection of officers during the early sessions specified that the president and main committee chairs should come from one of the smaller powers, these offices spread among the regional groups, and all of the Permanent Five included among the vice presidents. Thus the other members shared leadership of the General Assembly while the Permanent Five set the tone in the Security Council. Elections of assembly officers and main committee chairs have been governed by an explicit share-out among the five regional groups since 1958. The current sharing gives the African group six offices, the Asian group six, the Latin American group five, the Eastern European group four, and the Western European and Other group six while the sixth main committee chair rotates among the African, Asian, and Latin American groups.[18] Some delegations have proposed duplicating the practice regarding the assembly presidency by establishing a set rotation of each main committee chair among the groups. Most have resisted this idea in favor of continuing the annual intergroup consultations about which group will provide the chair of which main committee.

Each main committee elects a chair, two vice chairs, and a rapporteur. The chair presides over committee meetings and co-ordinates or encourages the informal consultations on procedural and substantive questions necessary to its effective functioning. The vice chairs preside as needed, and in most committees also organize or promote informal discussions on agenda items assigned to their care. The rapporteur, assisted by the Secretariat, drafts the summaries of debates and explanations of committee drafts that comprise its reports to the plenary. In early sessions the rapporteur occasionally presided at meetings, but the 1971 decision to elect two vice chairs ended this practice. Together the four officers also form the main committee's bureau, adjusting the plan of work issued at the start of the session to accommodate developments and prodding the committee to meet the plenary's target date for completing work. Some interregional balance is maintained within the committee leadership through the understanding that the chair, each of the two vice chairs, and the rapporteur will be drawn from a different regional group.

The assembly president has three roles – presiding impartially over plenary meetings, encouraging and sometimes even presiding over informal consultations among delegations or groups, and representing the General Assembly on ceremonial occasions. Main committee chairs have no representational role, but preside over meetings and encourage informal consultations in their committee.

General Assembly rules of procedure resemble those used in national legislative bodies, and at first glance give the presiding officer considerable authority to guide the conduct of the meeting. As in national legislatures, these grants of authority are balanced by specifying certain rules that cannot be ignored and permitting a majority of delegates to sustain an objection to the presiding officer's decision. Presiding officers do not push their authority very far for several reasons. They can be overruled by the body and do not like risking rebuff. As short-timers they do not want to create precedents that may limit their own scope for maneuver when they serve as national delegates in later sessions. They also believe that keeping a low profile preserves their ability to act as "honest broker" in the informal consultations. Yet they realize that failing to handle procedural motions and points of order expeditiously can create considerable confusion.[19] The wisest know that "expeditiously" does not always mean immediately. On many occasions letting more delegates speak than is allowed in the rules on debating procedural motions permits the presiding officer to assess the collective mood and make a generally supported procedural suggestion that facilitates orderly deliberation. Much depends on personal skill and tact, and at least one study attributes an increase in delegates' willingness to adopt procedural reform to particularly weak leadership from the president of the 33rd (1978) session.[20]

Increased use of informal consultations has made some parts of the presider's job easier. Most elections are now settled beforehand, with each regional group informing the president of its candidates, and the president reading out a consolidated list of endorsed candidates for assembly approval. Unlike in early sessions, when contested elections often required several ballots to resolve, balloting now occurs only when a regional group cannot agree on a candidate and two or more members compete. In the 1940s and 1950s, presiding officers often did not know what motions would be made or what proposals advanced at a particular meeting. By the early 1960s, informal consultations usually settled matters in advance.[21]

That same reliance on informal consultations has made other parts of the presider's job more demanding. Promoting informal discussions was such an important part of a main committee chair's job by the late 1970s that the vice chairs were being assigned to facilitate the consultations on particular items before the committee.[22] Assembly vice presidents later acquired a similar role. The president or chair also needs to determine ahead of time how the members want to adopt a draft resolution. They can use any of the several formulas for adoption without a vote ("by consensus," "by acclamation," "without objection," or "without a vote"), they can take a vote (only the total numbers tallied), or take a recorded vote (each member's individual vote is reported as well). As each draft to be adopted comes up, the presider reads its name and document number, then either calls a vote or announces that unless there is objection the draft will be considered adopted by the particular formula chosen. Occasionally, mixed-up messages or last-minute developments lead to an objection and then a vote; usually the presider declares the proposal adopted after a brief silence.

In the late 1940s there was some support for the idea that the assembly president would personify "the UN," but this never happened.[23] Dag Hamarskjöld (served 1953–61) drew personifying the organization into the Secretary-General's job where it has remained. The assembly president speaks "for the assembly" on ceremonial occasions, and has a separate page on the UN website, but remains far overshadowed by the Secretary-General. Main committee chairs sometimes speak for their committees in the plenary, but usually the rapporteur introduces the committee report and the draft resolutions it recommends.

Observers

The General Assembly also includes "observers," representatives from entities granted the right to attend meetings who sit at the back of the main floor behind national delegates rather than in the public or press galleries, receive all UN documents, and occasionally address a main committee or the plenary. Initially observer status was granted only to states that were not members of the UN, the Vatican (an entity the non-Catholic members could view as a state), and regional intergovernmental organizations. In the 1950s the US-led majority used observer status to allow its half of divided states a foot in the UN door while stalemate over admission to membership continued. In the late 1960s the Third World majority began extending observer status to national liberation groups endorsed by the Organization of African Unity, of which the South West Africa People's Organization (SWAPO) was the most prominent. Its 1974 decision to include national liberation groups endorsed by the League of Arab States meant extending observer status to the Palestine Liberation Organization (PLO) as well. Meanwhile the number of intergovernmental organizations with observer status also increased, going from three (the Organization of American States, the Commonwealth, and the Arab League) in 1950 to 20 today.[24]

Observers have acquired additional privileges over the years. Starting in 1971 they were permitted to address the plenary when it was discussing an issue of particular concern to them. By the late 1970s, observers routinely addressed main committees, and particularly favored ones were allowed to make statements to the plenary after adoption of resolutions. Broad Third World support for creation of a Palestinian state has been reflected in the broad privileges accorded to representatives of the Palestine Liberation Organization.[25] The assembly's shift towards greater use of informal consultations allowed motivated observers to acquire a more active role when a regional or subregional group allowed them to participate in its group discussions and help write proposals. In the late 1970s everyone at the assembly knew that PLO representatives had this role and that strong Arab and African support meant that the Group of 77 would not accept any proposal regarding Palestine that the PLO opposed.[26]

NGO representatives

In 1945, there were approximately 1,000 private associations having members in three or more countries.[27] While some were nonpolitical, others like labor

unions, women's groups, and the various organizations of the peace movement were very interested in political questions. As in the League period,
their contacts with the political organs of the UN – the Security Council
and the General Assembly – were limited. The UN Charter made no provision for observers from nongovernmental organizations or other private
entities to attend assembly sessions; at most they could sit in the public
galleries like other individual spectators. None of the great powers was
particularly enthusiastic about NGO participation in 1945; strong lobbying
by NGOs and their advocates at the San Francisco Conference yielded only
the Charter Article 71 system of NGO "consultative status" permitting
interaction with the Economic and Social Council and its various subsidiary
bodies.[28]

Though UN specialized agencies in the 1940s and early 1950s, and UN-
sponsored global conferences in the 1960s and later, developed separate
systems for accommodating NGO observers, the General Assembly remained
more aloof. Observers from a few NGOs with relevant expertise were allowed
to attend, and occasionally to address, meetings of assembly subsidiary bodies.
The Fourth Committee routinely included NGO representatives as well as
individual local inhabitants in meetings organized as hearings on conditions
in particular colonies. In 1978, some NGO representatives were allowed to
address the plenary when it was meeting as a "committee of the whole"
during the First Special Session on Disarmament, but this did not establish a
permanent change.

The shape of contacts between the General Assembly and nonstate actors
did change during the 1990s even though governments explicitly rejected
proposals to give NGOs observer status in the assembly.[29] Though controversial in many circles, the assembly began to re-define its relations with
multinational corporations in 1992 by abolishing the UN Commission on
Transnational Corporations and its secretariat unit, which had treated them as
inimical to Third World development. "Business" was included among the
"social groups" that needed to participate in successful sessions of the
Commission on Sustainable Development. Some grumbled when Secretary-
General Annan brought business executives into his consultations on a Global
Compact along with labor and "civil society." On the whole, the assembly has
followed Annan's lead in permitting representatives of a variety of nonstate
entities to participate in certain special assembly events like the October
2003 roundtables comprising the "high level dialogue on finance for development" and forums preceding the September 2005 High Level Plenary
Meeting of the Assembly.[30]

Despite lack of formal observer status some NGOs have a significant
impact on assembly proceedings through connections with particular national
delegations or units of the Secretariat. When they do, they can operate as an

"insider" concurrently with their "outsider" efforts to spread ideas through public campaigns and media attention. Despite discussion in the UN reform literature of proposals to create some form of direct representation for the populations of member states, most NGOs interacting with the UN have not devoted much energy to securing observer status in the assembly. They have devoted more energy to maintaining continued inclusion in parallel forums of global conferences and follow-up mechanisms such as the UN Commission on Sustainable Development. Some have concluded that contacts with UN bodies or the UN Secretariat are not all that useful because UN bodies have little influence over member state policy; others prefer to remain "outsiders" relying more on public campaigns.

The UN Secretariat

Though formally servants of the organization and the member states, the more senior Secretariat officials directly involved in assembly proceedings often provide a guiding hand. Recent Secretaries-General have used their Annual Report on the Work of the Organization to launch proposals or suggest frameworks for discussion of the issues of the day. They have also commissioned reports on particular global issues from panels of eminent persons,[31] and used them (with varying success) as platforms for inspiring new discussions. The Secretary-General and the top budget officers are closely involved in the processes of drawing up budgets and considering expenditures. Different units of the Secretariat are asked to prepare reports and studies that, when not used as an excuse to dump an item off the agenda, also help channel consideration of particular issues. The chief officer attached to the assembly plenary, a main committee, or a subsidiary body is often the source of procedural suggestions. The Secretariat can also influence the course of events by how well it implements the terms of assembly resolutions.[32]

Outline of a General Assembly session

The General Assembly has three types of session. The annual regular session begins in mid-September, continues through about 22 December, and since 1978 has resumed every year for at least one day in the spring or early summer. Article 20 of the Charter specifies that special sessions can be convened on request of the Security Council or when a majority of the member states endorses a request by one or more member states. In practice, most special sessions are called by decisions made at an earlier regular assembly session. Emergency special sessions can be convened on 24 hours' notice under the procedures for rapid action established by the Uniting for Peace Resolution in 1950.[33] Because they have broader agendas, last longer, and produce the vast majority of assembly resolutions, the regular sessions follow the most elaborate procedures. Special and emergency special sessions focus on the particular issues that inspired convening them, and use simpler procedures.

Regular sessions: preliminary phase

The General Assembly's first order of business is to elect assembly and main committee officers, and select the nine states that will serve on the Credentials Committee. Until 2001, officers were elected at the start of the session in September; since then the president and main committee chairmen have been elected the previous June at a meeting of the resumed prior session.[34] Now the regular session starts with the annual General Debate. Unlike the general debates on particular agenda items, this is an occasion for each delegation to discuss whatever issues it wishes and present its government's views on the state of the world. To cope with the continuing pressure of a large agenda, the amount of meeting time allocated to the General Debate was reduced from three to two weeks in 2003 by limiting speakers to 15 minutes each.[35] Even with this limitation, many heads of government and ministers of foreign affairs speak for their countries in the General Debate because it provides a prominent platform for announcing new proposals and coming to New York offers an opportunity to meet many counterparts in one trip.

While the General Debate proceeds, the General Committee, consisting of the president, vice presidents, and main committee chairs, begins its work. Assembly rules 40, 41, 42, and 44 give it five tasks: 1) recommending whether an item should be included on the agenda, 2) suggesting allocations of items among the main committees and the plenary, 3) assisting the president in setting the agenda of each plenary meeting, 4) co-ordinating main committees' work, and 5) editing adopted resolutions to improve their form (subject to acceptance by the plenary). These rules could have been used to establish a strong steering committee such as existed in the League of Nations Assembly,[36] but the General Assembly explicitly rejected this path. In 1947 it amended rule 41 to specify that the General Committee "shall not, however, decide any political question" and in 1949 amended rule 40 to specify that it "shall not discuss the substance of any item except in so far as this bears upon" including the item on the agenda or determining which main committee should handle it.

The General Committee has never used its powers to the full. Most of the assembly agenda consists of items included by assembly decisions made at previous sessions. Specialization among the main committees is sufficiently strong that items on the agenda for more than one session are allocated to the same main committee unless they are shifted into the plenary for its direct consideration. Co-ordinating main committee schedules and prodding the laggard to catch up devolved to informal weekly meetings among the assembly president, the main committee chairs, and the UN under secretary-general in charge of assembly affairs.[37] The General Committee never attempted to edit resolutions, partly on arguments that it is difficult to know where editing ends and substantive alteration begins and partly because editing could easily undo the "intentional ambiguity"[38] that is often the basis of a consensus.

The General Committee does recommend the closing date for each session and has become more active in making general suggestions for the speedier flow of work in recent years. However, each main committee remains the master of its own work pattern within the timelines established for the session as a whole.

Regular sessions: substantive phase

Each main committee begins its substantive work with an organizational meeting, now occurring on about 28 September, to elect its vice chairs and rapporteur, formally receive the list of agenda items allocated to it, and adopt a preliminary schedule of work based on Secretariat suggestions. In earlier decades most main committees began work while the plenary continued its General Debate; today that Debate is brief enough that most wait until it has ended.

In October and November most of the assembly's work proceeds in the main committees. The General Assembly, like the League Assembly before it, began with six Main Committees: Political (First), Economic (Second), Social (Third), Trusteeship and Non-Self-Governing Territories (Fourth), Administrative and Budget (Fifth), and Legal (Sixth). A seventh, never given a number, began as a committee of the whole to address the Palestine Question in 1947, continued as the Ad Hoc Political Committee in 1948, and was made permanent as the Special Political Committee in 1956. The success of decolonization left the Fourth Committee with little work after 1975, and in 1993 it was merged with the Special Political Committee. Today, the assembly again has six main committees:

First Committee	–	Disarmament and International Security
Second Committee	–	Economic and Finance
Third Committee	–	Social, Humanitarian, and Cultural
Fourth Committee	–	Special Political and Decolonization
Fifth Committee	–	Administrative and Budgetary
Sixth Committee	–	Legal

The main committees are committees of the whole including members of every delegation for two reasons. First, the assembly inherited a strong international tradition that formal consideration of proposals in intergovernmental conferences or meetings should involve every delegation attending. Second, even if that tradition had been challenged in 1946, there was no party system or other way to divide the member states into mutually exclusive groups and assign some of the group to stand in for all as occurs in national legislatures. Yet a committee of 51, like one of 191, is too large for working out the details of decisions. The main committees have dealt with this problem by relying on smaller groups – formally established sub-committees, "contact groups," or "working groups" and informal discussions of various types – to work out the details of draft resolutions.[39] Main committees shift between formal public meetings and closed informal sessions as needed, and some even reserve certain days for informal sessions in their initial plans of work.[40]

October and early November are also the period when the plenary takes up the organizational matters and "hot issues" it has reserved to itself. Most of the resolutions and decisions adopted during these months address routine items such as selecting members for other UN bodies or noting the reports of other UN organs. The rest address the international controversies that one or more members believe deserve the added attention of being debated in the plenary hall. Main committees also expedite work on a "hot" issue if a majority has strong views on it. Thus the 1975 statement that "Zionism is a form of racism" was drafted in the Third Committee and adopted in the plenary on 10 November,[41] and the first round of resolutions condemning South African (until 1994) or Israeli actions appears in late October or early November.

Together the plenary and the main committees make the assembly seven bodies in one. Each main committee has developed a distinctive character and procedural practices over the years. These are based partly on differences in the substantive issues before the committee, and partly on the fact that any national delegation large enough to do so has its members specialize in a particular committee's work. Each main committee thus develops its own collective identity.

The First Committee was once the scene of the liveliest debates in the assembly. Many of the Cold War confrontations between the superpowers occurred there before shifting into the plenary. After its establishment, the Special Political Committee became a second venue for confrontational debates. In the 1950s and 1960s the two political committees had overlapping agendas, with items allocated between them as much by which one had the lighter agenda at the moment as by any substantive relation to the other items already being handled in each. However the Special Political Committee remained the primary forum for addressing the two political issues of greatest continuing interest to the African-Asian group at the core of the Group of 77: the Arab–Israeli/Palestinian–Israeli conflict and matters relating to South Africa and its apartheid policy. Rationalizing the division of labor between the two committees by allocating all questions of disarmament, arms control, and general measures to enhance international peace and security to the First Committee while concentrating discussion of particular conflicts in the Special Political Committee was proposed in 1971.[42] It was not adopted until 1978 when the First Committee was also given the task of monitoring the progress of disarmament programs adopted at the 10th Special Session (First Special Session on Disarmament).[43]

Specializing in disarmament, nuclear weapons-related issues, and human activity in outer space transformed the First Committee. Its work began to proceed in a relatively calm manner, with delegates competing in expressing their government's desire for peace. Some lengthy polemics did arise during the revival of superpower tensions during the early 1980s, but the sort of speech that inspires a delegation to insist on exercising its right of reply has been uncommon since the end of the Cold War. It and the UN Conference on Disarmament are the major forums where the non-nuclear weapons states continue their campaign to eliminate that class of weapons.

The Second and Third Committees always had some difficulty determining where the "economic" and the "social" divide; each developed a core area competence by focusing on different chapters of the Economic and Social Council's reports. As the Afro-Asian group coalesced in 1960 and Third World membership continued to grow, the agendas of both committees became larger as questions of economic development were referred to the Second Committee and questions of self-determination, elimination of racial discrimination, and social effects of development were referred to the Third.

The Second Committee gained at the expense of the limited-membership Economic and Social Council because the Group of 77 came to prefer discussing economic issues in forums where all UN member states are represented. This development was not slowed when the Third World was assured a majority on the Council by increasing its membership from 18 to 27 in 1963, or reversed by the further enlargement to 54 members in 1973. Only in the 1990s was there significant discussion of reviving the Economic and Social Council (see Chapter 4).

The Economic and Social Council was not similarly eclipsed on the social side of its work by the Third Committee. This owes something to the prominence of human rights issues, which were handled in ECOSOC subsidiary bodies. However, it also reflects another fact of political life. In the UN's earlier decades many heads of delegation regarded social issues as the least important part of the agenda, and hence the Third as the least important main committee. This attitude contributed to and may have been intensified by delegation assignments. The minority of national delegations that included women in the 1940s and 1950s usually assigned them to the Third Committee, making it the one part of the Assembly with significant female presence. As more national delegations included women in later decades, the Third Committee remained their usual assignment.[44] Even in 1991, the proportion of female delegates in the Third Committee was more than double that in any other.[45]

By 1970 the initial pattern of distinguishing between "economic" and "social" issues was breaking down, with overlapping discussions consuming considerable time. In 1971 the special committee on rationalizing the assembly heard but did not endorse proposals that the Second Committee address all aspects of development while the Third handle the expanding human rights agenda and particular problems (such as relief after natural disasters) requiring immediate attention.[46] This idea was not adopted at the time, but the two committees later moved in that direction.

The Second Committee continues to focus primarily on South–North issues. In the 1970s and 1980s it served as another forum, parallel to UNCTAD, where the Group of 77, with verbal Soviet bloc support, pressed demands that the UN system become an institution for redistribution of wealth from industrial to developing countries. Concurrently the Third Committee devoted most of its time to two sorts of human rights items. The first involved arguments about whether some proposed right or group of rights should be defined as a "human right," while the second focused on the human rights situation in a particular state. The Third World majority has used the Third Committee to develop resolutions condemning the human rights records of its favorite target states, and to shield states in its good graces from extensive criticism over human rights violations.

The evolution of the Fourth Committee has been driven by the success of decolonization. Administration of the minority of colonies placed within the UN Trusteeship System was supervised by the Trusteeship Council, while Chapter XI (Articles 73–4) of the Charter established the basis for General Assembly comment on the larger number of colonies outside Trusteeship. The Fourth Committee was anti-colonial from the start, though it foresaw a more gradual transition when the US-led majority controled it. The tone of committee proceedings became increasingly strident after the influx of new African members in 1960. The enlarged Afro-Asian group secured adoption of the Declaration on the Granting of Independence to Colonial Countries and Peoples (GA Resolution 1514 (XV) of 14 December 1960), which established independence as the preferred future for colonial peoples and created the Committee of 24 to oversee the process by inquiring more closely into each territory's progress to independence. Continuing decolonization reduced the number of territories on the Fourth Committee's agenda but increased its rhetorical stridency as the most stubborn cases – the Portuguese government's refusal to consider decolonization, South Africa's refusal to withdraw from administering Namibia, and the whites-only Ian Smith regime that derailed British plans to establish black majority rule in Rhodesia – came to dominate its agenda.

When a new government in Lisbon granted independence to Portuguese colonies in 1974–5 and the Smith regime was replaced by a black majority government in 1979, the Fourth Committee was left with a much shrunken agenda of Namibia and small island territories in the Caribbean and the Pacific. However, the radical Third World cluster controling the Committee of 24 kept the Fourth Committee busy by annual examination of conditions in those 18 territories, discussion of the activities of "foreign economic and other interests" said to impede the exercise of self-determination, and condemnations of Western imperialism and neocolonialism. The end of the Cold War and South African withdrawal from Namibia in 1990 took much of the impetus out of the old Fourth Committee, and the remaining colonial items are only part of the reconstituted Special Political and Decolonization Committee's agenda.[47]

The Fifth Committee supervises the general operations of the UN Secretariat, provides guidelines for policies on staff conditions and recruitment, works out the UN budget, settles the assessment each member must pay to support organization activities, and advises on the financial implications of any proposed assembly initiative requiring expenditures. It is assisted in these tasks by two committees of individual experts, the sixteen-member Advisory Committee on Administrative and Budgetary Questions (ACABQ) and the eighteen-member Committee on Contributions (CC). The ACABQ goes over the Secretariat's proposed budget and makes recommendations about whether particular items should be increased, accepted as proposed, or reduced. Discussion of budget estimates is a three-sided conversation among the Secretariat, which presents and explains its requests; the ACABQ, which adds its comments; and the Fifth Committee, which finalizes the spending plans. The assessment process begins with the Fifth Committee setting the rules for determining individual member states' assessments. This is always a source of lively debate because there are different ways to interpret the general rule that assessments should reflect a state's size and level of economic development by being based in large part on its economic production as a fraction of world production (see Chapter 4). Once the formula – which is readjusted every few years – is set, the CC takes the budget totals adopted by the assembly, apportions them according to the assessment formula, calculates the money amount of each member's assessment, and presents the results to the Fifth Committee. The committee then presents the resulting scale of assessments to the plenary.

Formal debates in the Fifth Committee tend to be focused and nonpolemical, but the committee has long been riven by strong tensions between the Third World majority and the group of industrial states paying the largest assessments. The former seeks higher regular budgets and greater funding of development assistance and other programs it desires while the latter opposes significant budget increases and dislikes certain majority priorities. Strong words do fly on one complaint, accusations that particular member states – mainly but not only the USA – are hobbling the organization by paying assessments late in the year or unfairly withholding money they are obliged to pay.

Most delegates in the Sixth Committee are experienced international lawyers who often feel that the committee's relatively short agenda – 11 items in 1977, 18 in 1985, and 16 in 2003 – underutilizes their talents. Successive studies of assembly reorganization have recommended greater use of the Sixth Committee for preparing multilateral treaties. However, member governments generally prefer using separate global conferences, other assembly bodies, or *ad hoc* forums that they regard as more open to political arguments and compromises.

Most Sixth Committee debates are measured comments on the legal issues that come before it. Criticism of other states' policies is usually indirect, focusing on weaknesses of the legal doctrines or the lack of congruence between their conduct and their professed beliefs. Though used in the past to develop some landmark assembly resolutions, like the 1970 Declaration of Legal Principles governing Friendly Relations and Co-operation among States,[48] the committee is now overshadowed by other negotiating forums.

By 1970, most main committees' workloads were heavy enough to elicit agreement that the assembly needed to "rationalize" its procedures. The main impetus for change has been the increasingly severe time pressure caused by the tension between members' desire to maintain an open assembly agenda and reluctance to drop any item from the agenda as long as even a small group of states wants it on the list.

What has been a very halting rationalization process began with the Fifth Committee, which was close to breaking down under the pressure of dealing with budget and staffing issues each year. The assembly eased its situation by deciding that from 1970 the UN budget would cover a two-year period,[49] allowing it to alternate between budget and staffing issues. The 1971 reform committee endorsed extending a similar "biennialization" of issues to other main committees, but the idea spread slowly. Experiments during the 25th (1970) and 27th (1972) were dropped, though the Second Committee resumed "biennialization" of several items in the late 1970s. In 1983, the assembly urged main committees to identify items that could be considered every other year, and instructed its subsidiary bodies to consider reporting every second year.[50] The First Committee, faced with a long list of issues a significant group wants considered each year, adopted a different method of rationalization. It reorganized its agenda into "thematic" clusters in which closely related items are debated together.[51]

Though spreading slowly in the 1980s, biennialization gathered momentum later as time pressures continued to mount. Work programs for the most recent sessions reflect decisions that certain items will be considered every second, third, or even fifth year. These variations in interval provide some indication of the priority the Third World attaches to the various issues that have been left on the agenda over the years. While reluctant to drop any issue, the Group of 77 is now prepared to admit that some do not need to be discussed as often.

Yet even with these new practices, the busier main committees struggle to meet the traditional schedule of reporting the bulk of their work to the plenary between 15 November and 5 December. By then the plenary has finished with the items it took up directly and, unless there is some late-breaking crisis requiring its attention, it devotes its meetings to considering the increasing flow of reports from the main committees. The pressure on main committees to complete their work is particularly severe regarding proposals for new spending commitments. These must be sent to the Fifth Committee by the end of the first week of December so it can consider the Secretary-General's statements of how much their adoption will cost and whether this cost can be accommodated within the current budget authorizations. The plenary cannot vote on the proposal until it has received the Fifth Committee's statement on financial implications.

Plenary meetings in December are rushed and seem rather perfunctory as main committee rapporteurs introduce and the plenary adopts 20 to 30 draft resolutions a meeting. In most cases, delegations simply endorse what has been agreed in main committee so they can end the session by 23 December. The pace only slows if there are new developments that need to be addressed or some delegations mount last-minute efforts to change what was agreed in committee. Securing last-minute changes is difficult,[52] but careful preparations can secure a sympathetic hearing.

During the UN's first quarter century, most regular General Assembly sessions ended in December. The existence of permanent missions in New York improved telecommunications, and the more rapid transportation provided by jet aircraft (1960 was the first year as many people crossed the Atlantic by airplane as by ship), all made it easier to resume a session in the spring. The Assembly got into the habit of doing so every year in the 1980s, and the resumptions become longer after 1991 as the increase in UN peace-keeping and conflict-resolution activities required the Fifth Committee to reassemble to consider all the draft resolutions on mission expenses. Even if the budgeting for those operations was consolidated and done in the fall, which seems unlikely, assembly rules now require resuming the session in June to elect the officers of the next session.

Special and emergency sessions

These sessions, called as needed, can last anywhere from one day to several weeks. They operate under streamlined procedures, with the same president, vice presidents, and main committee officers as the preceding regular session and a short agenda defined in the call for a session. Sometimes main committees will be convened; more often the matter at hand is considered in plenary with some preliminary discussion in committee of the whole. Emergency sessions react to developments, though draft resolutions likely to come before the recurring Tenth Emergency Special Session on "Illegal Israeli Actions in Occupied Territories" are now predictable. Some special sessions – like the 16th (1989) on "Apartheid and Its Destructive Consequences in Southern Africa" – address particular conflicts. Since the late 1970s most of them have been thematic discussions of a broad global issue – like the 10th (1978), 12th (1982), and 15th (1988) Special Sessions on Disarmament – or a follow-up to a UN-sponsored global conference – like the 21st (1999) on "Implementation of the Program of Action of the International Conference on Population and Development."

Agenda formation

Agenda formation in the General Assembly involves balancing between the open nominal agenda, giving each member state wide latitude in the choice of issues it raises, and the less extensive effective agenda, formed as the constraints of time force majorities to select the smaller set of issues given extended attention. Assembly rules and practices exert some influence over the issues that make it on to the effective agenda, but have far less impact than the political alignments among the membership. These alignments, particularly the composition of a stable majority, guide governments' perceptions of what issues, and what proposals for handling them, are likely to receive a sympathetic hearing and win majority endorsement.

Nominal agenda

Member governments regard the assembly's open agenda as "one of the most treasured aspects of the United Nations"[53] because it serves important political and organizational ends. Politically, it reinforces the principle of sovereign equality of states by putting all members on the same footing and helps maintain state freedom of action by providing assurance that they can bring their concerns to the assembly when, and in what, phrasing they choose. Organizationally, the open nominal agenda helps maintain assembly pre-eminence *vis-à-vis* all other UN bodies because they have limited subject matter competence. It also facilitates the assembly's forum functions by making it easy for even a relatively small state to bring up some issue or problem that it believes is not getting sufficient attention. Sometimes, as with Malta's 1967 suggestion to discuss exploitation of deep-seabed resources, the other members quickly perceive that importance; at other times, as with Grenada's 1977 suggestion to study "Co-ordination of Research into Unidentified Flying Objects and Related Phenomena," they persist in regarding the question as unimportant. The open nominal agenda also facilitates turning the assembly into an arena for conflict, whether to secure an endorsement for one's own position, to secure condemnation of the other side's position, or simply to get the matter aired in public whenever a majority is willing to listen.

The assembly's open nominal agenda is established in Article 10 of the UN Charter: "The General Assembly may discuss any questions or any matters within the scope of the present Charter or relating to the powers and functions of any organs provided for in the Charter and, except as provided in Article 12, may make recommendations to the Members, to the Security Council or to both on any such questions or matters." Since the preamble defines UN concerns in very broad terms, there are few substantive limits on what merits assembly attention.

The Charter's few limitations on assembly authority to adopt resolutions appear in Articles 12(1) and 11(2) defining the assembly's relation to the Security Council, and Article 2(7) defining the UN's relation to member states. Article 12(1) specifies that "while the Security Council is exercising in respect of any dispute or situation the functions assigned to it in the present Charter, the General Assembly shall not make any recommendation in regard to that dispute or situation unless the Security Council so requests." Article 11(2) reminds the General Assembly that it should refer a dispute initially brought to it to the Security Council if it decides that there is a need for collective action against one or more disputing states. Article 2(7) establishes a more general limit on assembly competence by specifying that "nothing contained in the present Charter shall authorize the United Nations to inter-vene in matters which are essentially within the domestic jurisdiction of any State or shall require the Members to submit such matters to settlement under the present Charter; but this principle shall not prejudice the application of enforcement measures under Chapter VII." None of these provisions have been amended, but successive interpretations have narrowed their impact over the years.

Article 12(1) does not affect assembly discussion; it only limits adoption of resolutions. Nor does it prevent the assembly from adopting resolutions addressed to all members, even if they contain suggestions relevant to resolving a particular dispute. The question of what resolutions the assembly can adopt becomes acute when the Security Council appears to be stalemated and members of the assembly want to step in with suggestions for handling the dispute. If, as foreseen in one part of the "Uniting for Peace" resolution,[54] a simple majority of the Security Council requests the General Assembly to take up a question, it can make pointed comment, name names, and give the disputants very specific suggestions.[55] More often, however, the council stalemates without explicitly transferring the issue to the assembly. On such occasions the assembly has to determine whether the council is still "exercising its functions." The Soviet bloc originally argued that the council is still doing so as long as it keeps an item on its agenda. Yet the Soviets happily joined the assembly majority deciding to take up the Suez Crisis in November 1956 even though the item was being debated in the council and no one had yet proposed any draft resolutions, much less seen them defeated by the expected British and French vetos.[56]

The second element of the Uniting for Peace resolution went further by permitting a majority of the assembly to convene an emergency special session of the assembly if the council does not meet or fails to adopt any resolutions. This track was first brought into play by the USSR when it requested that the assembly convene an emergency session to deal with the June 1967 Arab–Israeli War as soon as it became clear that the USA would veto Soviet proposals. The Third World majority then adopted the view that the assembly could take up any conflict or dispute in emergency session if the Security Council was not "actively" considering it.[57] In the Third World majority's view, then, the assembly can step in whenever needed. At the time this was partly a reaction to the council's relative inactivity during the Cold War, but it also provides a standing opportunity for assembly majorities to challenge great power vetoes when they so choose.

The Third World majority did make greater use of both emergency and regular sessions to discuss particular conflicts after 1960. It adopted its own resolutions regarding conflicts even when the Security Council had acted, addressed resolutions to the parties by name, and urged them to take particular steps. The groundwork for this more assertive stance was established in the Western-tolerated effort to pressure South Africa over apartheid.[58] However, as noted by nearly every study of UN reform, the assembly has not been keen to assert its authority under the Uniting for Peace resolution to organize peacekeeping or peace enforcement missions, or to recommend sanctions.[59] Staying out of Cold War conflicts was simple prudence. Both during and after the Cold War, many Third World states preferred keeping their own conflicts out of the UN, were often very divided in their reactions to others' conflicts, and generally reluctant to take up a conflict that would publicly reveal those divisions.

The Third World majority's willingness to let the Security Council take the lead is also related to differences in the assembly's and the council's authority *vis-à-vis* member states. Article 11(2) does not limit the assembly's activities but it does remind everyone that the assembly cannot invoke Chapter VII and order member states to take collective action. The assembly can produce a rough equivalent if enough member states take the actions it suggests, and this has happened when there were strong states in the majority. Examples include creation of UNEF I in 1956, and continuation of collective action after an initial Security Council authorization was not renewed in Korea in 1950 and in the Congo in 1961. The trade embargoes against South Africa, Rhodesia, and Portugal had very uneven effect. These examples point out the important fact that an assembly majority's suggestions have a significant impact on the course or resolution of a conflict only if they are implemented by states (disputants, others, or both) with sufficient economic or military capability to make a significant difference in the situation.

The Article 2(7) provision that neither the UN nor any member state may intervene in "matters which are essentially within the domestic jurisdiction" of other states has not kept anything off the General Assembly agenda. This conclusion was reached in 1946 not by trying to determine what matters are "essentially within domestic jurisdiction" but by defining the term "intervention" restrictively. In that year India proposed discussing South Africa's discrimination against people of Indian origin, and sought to increase support for assembly involvement by saying that the question was not "domestic" because South Africa was violating an India–South Africa agreement that covered at least some of the victims. However, most members ignored India's suggestion and maintained that the assembly could add the issue to the agenda because discussion cannot be equated to intervention. This wide definition of assembly authority to debate remains unchallenged; members who want to avoid having something discussed have to persuade others to leave it alone.

The results of this interpretation have been very uneven. Assembly majorities have been eager to discuss the domestic policies and internal actions of certain states outside the majority, while states within the majority have usually enjoyed more solicitude for their sovereignty. In the 1970s and 1980s this dynamic produced very selective condemnations, with certain target states criticized severely while other states engaged in activities that were similar – or even worse – escaped all attention. This pattern abated after the end of the Cold War, but not enough to reduce US neoconservatives' perceptions of "double standards" in operation.

Effective agenda

Assembly rules contain three provisions that might be used to limit the agenda: 1) General Committee authority to suggest that particular items be omitted from the agenda, 2) establishment of deadlines for submission of items, and 3) allowance of procedural motions challenging assembly competence to consider a particular item.

A simple majority in the General Committee can recommend deleting particular items, and its recommendation is sustained if a simple majority of the plenary agrees. Any stable majority with members in enough regional groups, like the US-led majority in the late 1940s and a united Third World after 1956, could control it and use it as a filtering device. However no stable assembly majority sought to do so, preferring instead to maintain the open agenda. By the 3rd session, the General Committee was simply including on the agenda anything proposed at least 30 days before the session opened. Proposals to give the General Committee greater authority over the agenda or to establish a separate agenda committee were rejected several times.[60] Even in the current discussions of "revitalizing" the assembly, members have done little. They agreed to develop thematic clusters for agenda items,[61] but the proviso that this would not affect how the assembly carries out its deliberations means that the reluctance to eliminate items remains undisturbed.

Both the US-led and the Third World majorities had good political reasons for not pruning the nominal agenda. The US government understood that allowing other members to bring their concerns to the General Assembly was part of the price for their support on Cold War issues. Reluctance to prune is much stronger among the Third World coalition for two reasons. Its emphasis on the principle of sovereign equality of states inhibits support for formal rules that would obviously select among agenda proposals. Pruning is also inhibited by the political reality that Third World cohesion is often maintained by simultaneously addressing the concerns of all its regional and subregional groups rather than arranging any priorities among them.

Assembly rules establish the potential for imposing deadlines for submitting agenda items by distinguishing among three clusters of items at regular sessions. Those proposed at least 60 days in advance of the session form the provisional list; those proposed less than 60 but at least 30 days in advance form the supplementary list; and those proposed later are additional items. Rule 15 specifies that additional items should be "of an urgent and important nature," but even they can be added by simple majority of the membership. Though deadlines for submitting additional items were set at the 2nd and 4th sessions,[62] this practice was not maintained at other sessions. Thus, additional items can be accepted at any time before final adjournment of the session. This permits governments seeking extra publicity to present their initiatives in General Debate speeches more likely to be covered by the major news services.[63]

At least on paper, there are stronger restrictions on what can be added to the nominal agenda of special and emergency sessions. Rules 8 and 9 provide that the initial agenda of a special or emergency session consists of the item or items specified in the request for the session. Adding new items once the special or emergency session begins requires a two-thirds rather than a simple majority. For emergency sessions, the formal rules specify that any additional items must refer to other crisis situations, but majorities have ignored that rule on occasion.[64]

The main committees serve as the primary mechanisms for rationing attention. Rule 99 specifies that each main committee determines its own work schedule, allowing it to decide both the order in which items will be addressed and the amount of meeting time devoted to each one. Decisions about work schedule are procedural questions, settled by a simple majority, letting any coalition able to muster 50 percent plus one of the votes to allocate and reallocate committee attention as the session proceeds. This decentralization has allowed different coalitions of members to control the agenda in different main committees. In the late 1950s, an anticolonial Afro-Asian and Latin American majority ran the Fourth Committee while the US-led Cold War coalition ran the First and Special Political Committees. Though its influence had been diluted elsewhere, the most radical wing of the Third World majority still controlled the Fourth Committee in the late 1980s.

Though rule 99 states that main committees should consider all the items allocated to them, it has never been understood to require adopting a resolution on each one. Items that attract little interest are buried by failure to report to the plenary. Items that divide a majority or on which consensus-building will take a long time are deferred to a later session or put aside for later revival by requesting a secretariat or expert study. Failing to discuss an item is less painful to its proponents than removing it from the agenda entirely, and a few interested members can persuade the Third World majority to leave an item on the nominal list despite lack of effective attention.

Decision-making rules

Decision-making in the General Assembly is a contest in which proponents of some political demand work to secure an assembly endorsement of their favored proposition. Prevailing in this contest requires proponents to secure enough support to overcome both those who oppose making any decision whatever and those who prefer a different decision. The multisided character of the contest means that proponents of a particular proposal can be frustrated in at least three ways. Their proposal may be defeated outright because it arouses so much opposition. It may attract sufficient support only after so much compromise that the final version bears little resemblance to the original formulation. It may be adopted, but linked to others during a log-rolling process in ways that limit or dilute its impact.

A deliberative body's formal rules and practices about decision-making shape the contest in three ways. They define the number of yes votes necessary to adopt a decision, and simultaneously the number of no votes sufficient to block adoption. They also define the extent and nature of opportunities to delay decision, press for compromise, or attempt to split an emerging majority by introducing rival proposals or amendments that would change the meaning of others' proposals. Finally, they provide members of the deciding body and interested onlookers with a standard for assessing the propriety of the decision. Decisions secured by violating the rules or taking what others view as abusive advantage of procedural short cuts are more likely to be questioned than decisions made in full accordance with the rules. Prudent majorities thus pay attention to the "how" as well as the "what" of the decisions they secure, something that is particularly important since the General Assembly is not a legislature with command over administrative machinery able to turn its decisions into effective political outcomes.

The General Assembly has two sets of rules for decision-making. The first, the formal voting rules established in the UN Charter and the rules of procedure, is majoritarian. The second, which has developed through practice, is consensual. The assembly now relies more heavily on consensus, but a coalition confident of its numbers will revert to voting either when it has decided at the outset to impose its preferred decision or when it decides to press on after efforts to reach consensus fail. The consensus rule, which requires that virtually all members support or at least not object seriously to a proposal, is used when supporters seek broad agreement. Broad agreement is particularly important if supporters are trying to establish some proposition as a general norm of international relations. Until the 1990s, a unanimous vote – one in which an overwhelming number of delegations vote yes while none vote no or abstain – was regarded as the strongest form of endorsement. Today many delegations regard adoption "by consensus" as a stronger endorsement than any vote.

The politics of both majoritarian and consensus decision-making are shaped by the institutional fact that each UN member state has one vote in the General Assembly. This gives the numerous very weak states among the membership much more importance than they have elsewhere, creating the potential for lack of congruence between a coalition's ability to win votes in the assembly and capacity to produce outcomes congruent with the recommendations thus adopted. This gap between decision and implementation casts a shadow over politics in the assembly by reminding the many weak members that they can accomplish little if strong states oppose.

Majoritarian rules

The General Assembly's formal rules for decision-making are specified in Article 18 of the UN Charter:

1   Each member of the General Assembly shall have one vote.
2   Decisions of the General Assembly on important questions shall be made by a two-thirds majority of the members present and voting. These questions shall include: recommendations with respect to the maintenance of international peace and security, the election of non-permanent members of the Security Council, the election of members of the Trusteeship Council in accordance with paragraph 1(c) of Article 86, the admission of new Members to the United Nations, the suspension of the rights and privileges of membership, the expulsion of Members, questions relating to the operation of the trusteeship system, and budgetary questions.
3   Decisions on other questions, including the determination of additional categories of questions to be decided by a two-thirds majority, shall be made by a majority of the members present and voting.

Two aspects of this provision – permitting simple majorities to identify additional occasions when a two-thirds vote is necessary for approval, and defining the phrase "present and voting" – permit redefining the amount of support needed to adopt a proposal.

Though Article 18 suggests that whole categories of questions should be defined as "important," decisions that something requires a two-thirds vote for adoption have always been made in an *ad hoc*, question-by-question fashion. While relying on some background notions regarding what is "important," motions to define a decision as requiring a two-thirds majority generally arise when a particular coalition doubts it can muster a majority against another group's proposal but believes it can raise a blocking third. This is most likely when a significant number of member governments are cross-pressured on the matter, as were several Western European states on the question of seating the communist government's delegates as representing China in the 1960s. Western European governments satisfied domestic opinion by instructing their delegates to vote in favor of accepting the communist government's delegates, but only after propitiating their US ally by agreeing that the decision required a two-thirds vote because they knew the USA could muster a blocking third without them.

Definition of "present and voting" has been settled for all votes, and exerts a systemic effect on assembly decision-making. The term "present" has always been defined as at the meeting when a vote is taken.[65] Assembly rules 67 and 108 specify that delegates representing a majority of member states must be present for votes. In a 191-member Assembly, the quorum for voting is 96 members. This creates the possibility that a minority of all members could adopt a decision. The potential for converting minorities of the membership into voting majorities is further enhanced by the assembly's definition of the phrase "and voting." General Assembly practices permit four different expressions of opinion: favoring, opposing, abstaining, and not participating.[66] The Assembly's long tradition of treating abstention and nonparticipation as "not voting" reduces the number of votes needed to attain a majority.[67] If the bare quorum of 96 members is present and abstention or nonparticipation are considered as voting, a simple majority is 49 and a two-thirds majority is 65. If ten of the 96 abstain, 86 are "voting," making 44 a simple majority and 57 a two-thirds majority. In practice, however, few resolutions are adopted with such small numbers of affirmative votes because everyone understands that they would have little political weight.

Consensus practice

Dispensing with formal votes is an old assembly practice; at the first session more than three-fourths of the 113 resolutions were adopted without a vote (see Table 3.3). Though the share dropped below one-third during the height of Cold War tensions in 1949–54, it rose afterward. More than half of the assembly's resolutions were adopted without a vote between 1975 and 1990, and more than 75 percent since 1991. The Soviet bloc supported using consensus, and even wanted it to be the main rule for subsidiary bodies – like the Committee on the Peaceful Uses of Outer Space and the 18-Nation Disarmament Committee – dealing with major political issues in the late 1950s and early 1960s, so it would have protection from the US-led majority. Though some Third World commentators would like to see the Assembly rely more on majority votes,[68] the Third World majority today accepts consensus for the same reason the US-led majority accepted it in the 1950s: states outside the majority coalition possess the capacity to frustrate realization of assembly recommendations they oppose.

The consensus rule practiced in the assembly and its main committees stands somewhere between the unanimity requirement in the League of Nations and the majoritarian rules of the UN Charter. Efforts to define the concept more clearly began in 1965 at the first meetings of the Special Committee on Peacekeeping Operations. Several members suggested that

Table 3.3: Adoption of assembly resolutions.

Session	Total	No vote (%)	Unanimous(%)	Two-thirds(%)	Simple majority (%)
1	113	89 (78.8)	4 (3.5)	19 (16.8)	1 (0.9)
2	81	47 (58)	1 (1.2)	32 (39.5)	1 (1.2)
3	129	52 (40.3)	3 (2.3)	71 (55.0)	3 (2.3)
4	108	23 (21.3)	10 (9.3)	75 (69.4)	0 (0.0)
5	144	29 (20.1)	10 (6.9)	103 (71.5)	2 (1.4)
6	121	19 (15.7)	7 (5.8)	92 (76.1)	3 (2.4)
7	122	27 (22.1)	2 (1.6)	92 (75.4)	1 (0.8)
8	106	30 (28.3)	0 (0.0)	75 (68.8)	1 (0.9)
9	108	27 (25.0)	1 (0.9)	80 (74.1)	0 (0.0)
10	93	37 (39.8)	2 (2.2)	54 (58.1)	0 (0.0)
11	131	41 (31.3)	1 (0.7)	88 (67.2)	1 (0.8)
12	109	42 (38.5)	3 (2.8)	62 (59.9)	2 (1.8)
13	126	52 (41.3)	3 (2.4)	69 (54.8)	2 (1.6)
14	128	43 (33.6)	9 (7.0)	75 (58.6)	1 (0.8)
15	148	68 (45.9)	14 (9.5)	65 (43.9)	1 (0.7)
16	130	68 (52.3)	6 (4.6)	55 (42.3)	1 (0.8)
17	131	67 (51.1)	9 (6.9)	55 (42.0)	0 (0.0)
18	125	71 (56.8)	2 (1.6)	52 (41.6)	0 (0.0)
19	–	–	–	–	–
20	150	75 (50.0)	4 (2.7)	69 (46.0)	2 (1.3)
21	136	63 (46.3)	3 (2.2)	68 (50.0)	2 (1.4)
22	139	59 (42.4)	14 (10.8)	64 (46.0)	1 (0.7)

Continued on page 76

Table 3.3 continued

Session	Total	No vote (%)	Unanimous (%)	Two-thirds (%)	Simple majority (%)
23	142	57 (40.1)	15 (10.6)	69 (48.6)	1 (0.7)
24	158	64 (40.5)	5 (3.2)	87 (55.1)	2 (1.3)
25	160	58 (36.3)	2 (1.2)	98 (61.3)	2 (1.2)
26	180	55 (30.6)	11 (6.1)	114 (63.3)	0 (0.0)
27	177	56 (31.6)	12 (6.8)	109 (61.6)	0 (0.0)
28	181	73 (40.3)	4 (2.2)	104 (57.5)	0 (0.0)
29	187	95 (50.8)	5 (2.7)	85 (45.5)	2 (1.1)
30	215	119 (55.3)	4 (1.9)	89 (41.4)	3 (1.4)
31	251	158 (62.9)	3 (1.2)	90 (35.9)	0 (0.0)
32	262	158 (60.3)	6 (2.3)	98 (37.4)	0 (0.0)
33	274	155 (65.6)	5 (1.5)	113 (41.2)	1 (0.4)
34	299	185 (61.9)	0 (0.0)	113 (37.8)	1 (0.3)
35	317	187 (59.0)	0 (0.0)	128 (40.4)	2 (0.6)
36	333	193 (58.0)	1 (0.3)	138 (41.4)	1 (0.3)
37	345	190 (55.1)	2 (0.6)	152 (44.1)	1 (0.3)
38	323	178 (55.1)	0 (0.0)	145 (44.9)	0 (0.0)
39	350	201 (57.4)	0 (0.0)	149 (42.6)	0 (0.0)
40	356	210 (58.9)	0 (0.0)	145 (40.9)	1 (0.2)
41	309	159 (51.5)	1 (0.3)	148 (47.9)	1 (0.3)
42	318	172 (54.1)	1 (0.3)	145 (45.6)	0 (0.0)
43	324	184 (56.8)	0 (0.0)	140 (43.2)	0 (0.0)
44	335	206 (61.5)	0 (0.0)	129 (38.5)	0 (0.0)

Continued on page 77

Table 3.3 continued

Session	Total	No vote (%)	Unanimous (%)	Two-thirds (%)	Simple majority (%)
45	335	252 (75.2)	0 (0.0)	83 (24.8)	0 (0.0)
46	297	222 (74.7)	0 (0.0)	75 (25.3)	0 (0.0)
47	302	226 (74.8)	0 (0.0)	76 (25.2)	0 (0.0)
48	317	253 (79.8)	0 (0.0)	64 (20.2)	0 (0.0)
49	313	247 (78.9)	0 (0.0)	65 (20.8)	1 (0.3)
50	311	239 (76.8)	0 (0.0)	71 (22.8)	1 (0.3)
51	293	220 (75.1)	2 (0.7)	69 (23.5)	2 (0.7)
52	306	237 (77.4)	0 (0.0)	67 (21.9)	2 (0.7)
53	337	271 (80.4)	0 (0.0)	66 (19.6)	0 (0.0)
54	338	270 (79.9)	0 (0.0)	66 (19.5)	2 (0.6)
55	327	261 (79.8)	0 (0.0)	65 (19.9)	1 (0.3)
56	387	319 (82.4)	0 (0.0)	68 (17.6)	0 (0.0)
57	305	231 (75.7)	0 (0.0)	74 (24.3)	0 (0.0)
58	316	244 (77.2)	0 (0.0)	69 (21.8)	3 (0.9)

"consensus" should be equivalent to the assembly definition of a unanimous vote as one in which there are no negative votes or abstentions whether or not the total of positive votes is less than the total UN membership.[69] Others were not ready to adopt that strict a definition. By 1974, the main elements of the current definition were in place, and consensus understood to mean general agreement without a vote but not necessarily unanimity.[70] Yet there remained some disagreement about what this meant. The Soviet bloc insisted that it should mean agreement across the three main ideological "camps" of the world – socialist, capitalist, and nonaligned. Others defined it as wide agreement within and between the five regional groups, a definition subsuming the Soviet approach because the divisions among regional groups largely paralleled those between ideological camps during the Cold War.

Decision by consensus was endorsed, but not suggested as a replacement for voting in the 1971 study of General Assembly procedures: "The Special

Committee considers that the adoption of decisions and resolutions by consensus is desirable when it contributes to the effective and lasting settlement of differences, thus strengthening the authority of the United Nations. It wishes, however, to emphasize that the right of every Member State to set forth its views in full must not be prejudiced by this procedure."[71] Yet it was not until after both the Third World and West reconsidered their positions after the highly contentious 6th Special Session on Raw Materials and Development in 1974 that the proportion of resolutions adopted without a vote again exceeded 50 percent.

Like requiring a two-thirds vote, adoption by consensus involves recruiting a "supermajority" for adoption of a decision. Requiring a supermajority gives some advantage to the status quo, whether that status quo is an absence of any policy or a previously adopted policy that some members now hope to alter. The assembly definition of the phrase "present and voting" reduces the size of the necessary supermajority in formal voting, but reliance on consensus increases it.

In the 1970s the assembly began making a distinction between adoption "by consensus" and adoption "without a vote" or "without objection." The term "by consensus" indicated that every delegation had been involved to some extent in negotiation of the resolution and identified positively with it while the other terms indicated that some delegations were willing to let others adopt the proposal without having any enthusiasm for it themselves. Though some outside observers dismiss the "consensus"/"without a vote"/"without objection" distinction as having no meaning outside the General Assembly hall,[72] delegates pay attention.

The simultaneous availability of majority voting and consensus adoption allows delegations to express gradations of support for or opposition to any particular proposal. Adoption "by consensus" or on a unanimous vote indicates very broad and strong support; widespread but less strong support is expressed by "adoption without objection" or "adoption without a vote." Voting indicates some opposition, the amount of opposition increasing as the result goes from a small number of abstentions to a large number of abstentions, to abstentions and isolated negative votes, and finally to abstentions and large numbers of negative votes.

Year-by-year variations in adoption of resolutions dealing with human rights in, or aid to particular countries indicate how other governments are reacting to developments in that country or the shifting limits of agreement on the extent to which the international community should be specifying standards of domestic behavior. Similarly, individual delegations can signal the contours of their country's policy in considerable detail when an issue inspires multiple proposals at the same session. Western governments signaled how far they were willing to go in taking action against South Africa or Israel by joining in consensus adoption of some resolutions, asking for a vote to abstain on some, and asking for a vote to vote against others. Similar patterns have developed on resolutions dealing with disarmament and economic development, with different delegations supporting, going along with, or objecting to different resolutions. These variations tell delegates what proposals will and will not provide good platforms for developing further proposals along the same lines in future sessions.

Deliberation, negotiation, and grandstanding

The General Assembly's deliberative functions occur in two distinct places: the meeting halls where formal speeches and other remarks are recorded in written minutes, and the lounges, corridors, conference rooms, mission offices, and social gatherings where informal discussions proceed. The assembly rules of procedure regulate the public meetings and allow shifting discussions to informal settings as needed; unwritten practices channel the informal discussions.

Even when informal discussion predominates, public debate in the assembly serves several functions. The first three are common to all deliberative bodies. Public debate gives supporters a chance to explain the rationale for their proposal and outline the consequences they expect or hope will follow from its adoption. This is particularly important when groups or individuals who are not members of the decision-making body must help implement the decision or can exercise influence over other members. Similarly, public debate gives opponents a chance to offer their reasons for objecting. More generally, public debate is the mechanism through which all members can maintain the political conversation over time, allowing for reconsideration when decisions do not have the anticipated effects, conditions change, or new ideas take hold. Assembly public debates also reaffirm the principle of sovereign equality of the members by giving each an equal chance to express its views.

Formal rules and informal practices also guide using the assembly as an arena. While quiet "corridor diplomacy" at UN Headquarters is often used to help settle problems, the assembly's public meetings allow parties in a conflict to advance their claims, criticize other parties' claims, and seek support from other governments by appeals to their delegates or to public opinion through media publicity. Public meetings also permit individual or collective displays of strong emotion.[73] These include Soviet Premier Khrushchev banging his fists and his shoe to reinforce his points in September 1960, eliciting a gavel-breaking attempt to call him to order by the assembly president on one occasion and a cooler "I should like that to be translated if he wants to say anything" from the interrupted British Prime

Minister Macmillan on another.[74] In 1974, PLO Chairman Arafat caused considerable stir when his gesturing during a November 1974 speech to the plenary revealed a holster under his belt.[75] Third World delegates have used collective responses to register defiance of great powers on several occasions. These include shouts of approval plus thunderous and prolonged applause after Secretary-General Hammarskjold declined Soviet demands that he resign in October 1960,[76] leaping to their feet to applaud and some to dance after adoption of the resolution seating PRC delegates in October 1971,[77] applauding when the USA was left off the ACABQ in 1996,[78] and withholding all applause after US President George W. Bush addressed the assembly in September 2003.[79]

Public debate

Assembly rules of procedure bear strong resemblance to those used in national legislatures and other deliberative bodies. They divide formal debate on each individual agenda item into three phases. The first is a general debate in which delegations present their definition of the problem, their sense of its significance, and their ideas about how to address it. Next comes detailed examination of draft resolutions in which delegations comment on the merits or shortcomings of the draft or suggest refinements to the text that will, in their view, clarify what is intended or make it acceptable to more governments. The last phase consists of explanations of vote indicating why a particular delegation or group of like-minded delegations supports, opposes, or remains ambivalent about the resolution adopted.

Delegates to the assembly's early sessions participated in a very formal body guided almost entirely by the written rules of procedure. Each item referred to a main committee was debated twice, first in the committee and then (sometimes in abbreviated form) in plenary. When controversy arose, amendments and alternate proposals were presented to the meeting and debated in detail at public sessions. There were no general limits on the number or length of speeches each delegation could make, though individual meetings might decide to close debate or impose time limits on individual speeches. Most of the time, delegates could orate at length if they chose and much meeting time was taken up with the raising and challenging of various procedural motions.

The formal rules barely worked in the 1940s, and the combination of increasing UN membership plus longer agendas forced the assembly to streamline its working methods. New rules reducing the amount of time taken up with procedural debates were adopted in the 1950s, but few of the opportunities for obstruction were closed.[80] By 1960 members had tacitly agreed to limit themselves to one speech each in the plenary General Debate. They explicitly limited each plenary General Debate speech to 30 minutes in 1963, and to 15 minutes in 2003.[81] Also in the course of the 1960s, delegates became more willing to dispense with general debate on individual agenda items in the plenary that had been debated in a main committee. Though resisted earlier by the Soviet bloc, the move was accepted because it freed plenary time for consideration of the increasing number of security, political, and economic issues that the Third World majority wanted to take up there rather than in the less prominent forum of a main committee.

Change did not go much further until the press of members and issues forced even the Soviet bloc, always reluctant to impose limits on debate for fear this would reinforce the disadvantages of its minority status, to relent and accept the need for change in the assembly's procedures. As a Polish delegate explained:

> Members of the UN must retain the right to express themselves fully on agenda items allocated to main committees. On the other hand, the Organization now had 127 members, and all of those wishing to speak should be given an opportunity to do so. Situations frequently arose in which this was not possible, and some limitation on the length of statements was then obviously desirable in order to facilitate the more efficient of the available time.[82]

However, getting the assembly to adopt many of the recommendations took the rest of the decade. By 1979, when 149 members faced a 140-item agenda, delegations were limiting themselves to one 10 minute explanation of vote on each resolution reported from a main committee, to be delivered either that committee or the plenary, unless they had changed their vote in the mean time.

Other proposals have languished. Though each member gets only one opportunity to speak in the plenary General Debate, a similar limit has never been imposed in general debates on particular items, and adopting it now would reverse the momentum towards clustering related items for a "thematic" debate. Only in the busier committee has imposing standing time limits of 10 to 15 minutes for individual speeches been adopted. The process of settling the list of speakers, which indicates who wishes to speak on an item, has been expedited. At the first sessions the speaker's list remained open until the last speaker had finished, making it possible to sign up to speak again even if debate had already gone past the amount of time suggested in the committee or plenary workplan. In the 1970s, the list was closed at the end of the last meeting allocated to the item in the plan of work, which limited the overflow somewhat. In recent years the deadline has usually been the end of the first day during which the item is scheduled for consideration, forcing delegations to decide much earlier whether they intend to speak.

In sum, the days when a single delegate could tie up a meeting for hours with long presentations on a complex issue or with rambling remarks are long gone. Effectiveness in the public debate now depends on ability to convey views and ideas succinctly, and following the debate requires paying close attention since the speeches are set pieces rather than parts of an interactive conversation.

Main committees also moved away from the rigid taking up of items one at a time in the order listed in the late 1950s. Some began scheduling two items for the same meeting so that if work on one was interrupted for any reason the committee could turn its attention to the other. Others became more flexible about starting debate on another item when a working group was set up to develop a more widely acceptable proposal on the item just discussed. By the mid-1980s almost all discussion of the particular language to be incorporated into draft resolutions had been shifted to informal discussions. These changes meant that the order in which items were listed had little effect on the amount of attention they received. On the positive side, isolated delegations can no longer snarl the proceedings in a thicket of procedural motions. On the negative side, formal debates are sometimes very tangled and enough key choices made in unrecorded informal meetings that those outside the assembly often have difficulty understanding its deliberations.

Increasing use of informal discussion

The streamlined world of recent sessions, in which general debates and explanations of vote are much shorter and few alternative proposals are compared in detail in public session, is more the result of greater reliance on informal consultations than of changes in the formal rules of procedure. In the early sessions public meetings outnumbered informal sessions. Though some clusters of members – the Latin American group, the Soviet bloc, the Commonwealth and the Nordic states – often consulted among themselves, intergroup consultations were infrequent. Disagreements over details and procedure were raised and debated at length in formal meetings. This was partly the carryover of habits from older diplomatic practice, but also promoted by the desires of both the US-led majority and the Soviet bloc minority to use the assembly as a sounding board in their Cold War competition.

Secretariat efforts to encourage greater use of informal consultation[83] began to bear fruit in the late 1950s as members settled more procedural questions ahead of time and used working groups or *ad hoc* subcommittees to develop mutually acceptable draft resolutions. The reshuffling of regional groups triggered by the expansion of UN membership in the early 1960s led them to play a greater role in the informal discussions. With a membership growing further beyond 100 each year, it was clearly impossible to include every member in every informal consultation. The regional and other caucusing groups provided mechanisms for linking the delegations included to those remaining outside. This development was particularly helpful to smaller Third World members unable to afford sending a large delegation to New York each year and therefore dependent on regional counterparts for information and advice.

The changes in assembly process brought about by greater use of informal consultation were most visible in the second stage of consideration, the development of draft resolutions. In the 1960s contending clusters of sponsoring delegations typically submitted draft resolutions fairly early in the general debate on an item, a practice encouraged by the rule 91 stipulation that all proposals not withdrawn by their sponsors will be put to a vote in order of submission unless a majority decides otherwise. Only after formal submission did each group of sponsors reveal whether it was ready to work with others on developing a joint draft or would press for a vote on its own proposal regardless of others' reactions. Practice evolved further as delegations realized that considerable time could be saved if sponsors of rival drafts consulted each other about the possibility of developing a common draft.

The two patterns of consensus formation still visible today emerged in the 1970s. In the first, several draft resolutions are submitted early in consideration of an item, and withdrawn in favor of a consolidated text. In the second, formal debate is followed by informal negotiations and submission of a single draft resolution. In these situations, all that remains of the middle phase of formal debate is oral introduction of the draft.

The shift to greater use of consensus has often shortened the last phase of public debate – explanations of vote – as well, because a consensus resolution is already fairly noncontroversial. Many explanations of vote are joint statements made by one delegation on behalf of a regional or caucusing group. Individual delegations can still offer their own explanations, but are more likely to do so if the resolution is adopted by vote. The rule that explanations are given either in main committee or in the plenary, but not both, saves time but also means that many of the explanations are buried in the committee records.

The submission of only one draft is not always a sign of consensus. It can mean that a majority has coalesced around a particular proposition and is ready to force a vote when others object to it. This became the predominant pattern with resolutions about South African administration of Namibia, South African policies of apartheid, Israeli practices in occupied territories, and reports of the Committee on the Exercise of the Inalienable Rights of the Palestinian People in the 1970s. It continues with most resolutions on the Palestinian–Israeli conflict today. The political effect of such decisions depends very much on what the majority hopes will happen next, a subject of Chapter 4.

Whether proceeding formally or informally, the politics of securing adoption of a proposal is quite similar. Whenever the assembly is dominated by a stable majority, members in good standing with their caucusing group have an easier time advancing their proposals than do others. Delegations in the Third World majority typically seek endorsement from their regional group, and then build outward to the rest of the G-77 because traditions of mutual deference mean the whole group is unlikely to take up something opposed by a majority in a region. A cross-region caucus, like the Arab states with members in both the African and Asian groups, can potentially recruit a wider set of initial supporters. For delegations outside the Third World majority, winning majority support for a proposal requires finding Third World delegations willing to express their support – or even become formal co-sponsors of the draft – early in the negotiating process.

Public debate as arena

Use of the General Assembly as an arena for criticizing rivals and appealing to wider audiences began in earnest as the Second World War allies divided into contending Cold War blocs. Public debate provided both sides with occasions for asserting the superiority of its own vision for the world and the inferiority of the other's. By 1950, another broad cleavage, between an anti-colonial majority and the remaining colonial powers, had also emerged, but did not inspire the same two-way intensity of discussion because the colonial powers were more defensive and subdued. From the late 1960s through the 1980s, the South–North cleavage produced sharp rhetoric as the more radical members of the Third World coalition took the lead in denouncing Western imperialism and neocolonialism.

Assembly debates can also be used by participants to present their views of a more localized conflict. In the 1970s debates about Arab–Israeli and Palestinian–Israeli issues became many-on-one verbal slugfests as Arab and African delegations competed in the vehemence of their criticisms of Israel (or, as many of them still prefer to call it, "the Zionist entity") and Israeli delegates responded with equal vigor. The tone dampened occasionally in later years, but has returned to its old sharpness since the second Palestinian *intifada* began in September 2000. Exclusion of South African delegates from the assembly between 1974 and 1994 (see Chapter 4) meant sharp denunciations of apartheid and other South African policies were not vigorously challenged. Iranian and Iraqi delegates exchanged many a barb during their countries' 1980–8 war, helping persuade most members to relegate speeches in right of reply to the end of the meeting.

Using the assembly as an arena for conflict differs from using it as a deliberative forum mainly in the greater willingness to single out particular members for criticism and employ sharper rhetoric. Every assembly resolution projects some view of the world by explicitly or implicitly favoring some principles and norms or some courses of action over others. Actors supporting the disfavored principles and norms or engaging in the disfavored courses of action are being criticized more or less sharply depending on the terms of the resolution. When the assembly's public meetings are used to call wider attention to a conflict, to secure resolutions supporting one's own side, or to secure resolutions criticizing the other side, partisanship comes out into the open. Names are named, and the often vexing problem of how to apply generally accepted abstract principles in a particular situation is raised explicitly.

Procedural change as a reaction to more members and more issues

Assembly procedures have shifted from entirely formal to increasingly informal and assembly decision from mostly majoritarian to mostly consensual as the national delegates, both individually and in their regional and other caucusing groups, have sought to accommodate the realities of a growing membership and increasingly long agendas. The question of whether these responses are adequate will be explored in Chapter 5. First, however, it is necessary to examine what happens after the assembly adopts a resolution. Only by understanding the impact of assembly resolutions on the implementation phase of politics is it possible to assess the strengths and weaknesses of the institution and anticipate its future.

Notes

1 The current version is contained in UN Document A/520/Rev. 15 (1986) plus Amend. 1 (21 August 1991) and Amend. 2 (8 October 1993).
2 Distributed as Supplement 1 of the assembly records each year and accessible at www.un.org/ga/[session number]/documentation/. This is a relatively recent practice. Secretary-General Hammarskjold issued his annual reports in October.
3 UN Doc. ST/SG/SER.C/613, 7 October 2004.
4 Edvard Hambro, "Some notes on parliamentary diplomacy," in Wolfrang Friedmann *et al* (eds), *Transnational Law in a Changing Society* (New York: 1972), 287.
5 In 1950, delegates relied on the telegraph; a 3 mniute phone call from New York to London cost £9 ($25.00). Today phoning anywhere in the world costs a few cents a minute and missions can maintain e-mail for $40.00 or less a month.
6 Margaret Burton, *The Assembly of the League of Nations* (Chicago: 1941), 100–1.
7 See Bruce Brown, "Summary: a mid-life crisis for the UN at fifty," in Ramesh Thakur (ed.), *Past Imperfect, Future Uncertain* (New York: 1998), 250–1.
8 Sally Morphet, "States groups at the United Nations," in Paul Taylor and A.J.R. Groom (eds), *The United Nations at the Millennium: The Principal Organs* (London: 2000), 264.

9   Morphet, "States groups at the United Nations," 228; also see Angel Eduardo Zuleta, "How Latin America shaped the UN," *Americas* 34(5) (September–October 1982).

10 See Robert A. Mortimer, *The Third World Coalition in International Politics* (New York: 1980); Richard L. Jackson, *The Nonaligned, the UN, and the Superpowers* (New York: 1983); Andemacil.

11 In 2005 the Nonaligned has 114 members, and the G-77 has 134. On evolution of the G-77 see Charles A. Jones, *The North–South Dialogue: A Brief History* (London: 1983); Nigel Harris, *The End of the Third World: Newly Industrializing Countries and the Decline of an Ideology* (Harmondsworth: 1987); South Commission, *The Challenge to the South* (London: 1990).

12 Explanation by the President in UN Doc. A/19/PV.1286 (1 December 1964), par. 7–8.

13 Described in Peter R. Baehr, *The Role of a National Delegation in the General Assembly* (New York: 1970), 33–5.

14 E.g. Thomas Hovet, *Bloc Politics in the United Nations* (Cambridge, MA: 1960); Miguel Marin-Bosch, *Voting in the General Assembly* (The Hague: 1998).

15 David M. Malone, "L'affrontement Nord–Sud aux Nations Unies: un anachronisme sur le declin?" *Politique etranger* 68(1): 151 (spring 2003).

16 Sally Morphet, "Multilateralism and the global South," *Global Governance* 10(4): 517–37 (2004).

17 High Level Panel on Threats, Challenges, and Change, *A Secure World: Our Common Responsibility* (New York: 2004), par. 251. The Panel used this scheme in proposals for reforming the Security Council, and said it was not a suggestion regarding the General Assembly.

18 GA Resolution 47/233 of 17 August 1993.

19 See the discussions recorded in A/SPC/15SR.198 (11 November 1960), par. 14–25, and SR.199 (14 November 1960), par. 1–5; A/24/PV.1812 (19 November 1969), par. 42–102; and PV.1813 (19 Nov. 1969), par. 1–182 for good examples.

20 Keith Krause, W. Andy Knight and David Dewitt, "Canada, the United Nations, and the reform of international institutions," in Chadwick Alger, Gene M. Lyons, and John E. Trent (eds), *The United Nations System: The Policies of Member States* (Tokyo: 1995), 138.

21 Muhammad Zafrulla Khan, "The President of the General Assembly of the United Nations," *International Organization* 18(2): 234–5 (spring 1964), noted that he never faced an unanticipated request for a ruling from the chair during the 17th session.

22 For example the organizational discussion in A/C.3/34/SR.3 (24 September 1979), par. 7.

23 Yuen-li Liang, "Notes on legal questions concerning the United Nations," *American Journal of International Law* 55: 711 (1955).

24 List in UN Doc. A/INF/58/6 (19 December 2003).

25 GA Resolutions 42/177 of 15 December 1988 and 52/250 of 7 July 1998.

26 Erik Suy, "The status of observers in international organizations," Hague Academy of International Law *Recueil des cours* 160: 75–180 (1978).

27 Union of International Associations, *Yearbook of International Organisations* 4th ed., 1951–2.

28 Harold K. Jacobson, "Labor, the UN, and the Cold War," *International Organization* 11: 55–67 (1957); Pei-heng Chiang, *Nongovernmental Organizations at the United Nations: Identity, Role, and Function* (New York: 1981), 45–8.

29 See Decision 49/426 of 9 December 1994 and discussion in A/C.6/49/SR.10 (1994).

30 Each roundtable involved ministerial-level participants from governments, two or three "representatives of civil society," and two or three from the "business sector." See UN Doc. A/58/436, par. 23–5 (15 October 2003) and GA Resolution 59/145 (17 December 2004).

31 Such as the Jackson Report, *A Study of the Capacity of the United Nations Development System* (UN Doc. DP/5, 1969); the Brandt Commission report, *North–South, A Program for Survival* (Cambridge, MA: 1983); the Bruntland Commission Report, *Our Global Neighborhood* (Oxford: 1995).

32 See Leon Gordenker, *The UN Secretary-General and the Secretariat* (London: 2005) for additional discussion.

33 GA Resolution 377(V) of 3 November 1950.

34 GA Resolution 56/509 of 8 July 2001 for election of the president and vice presidents; GA Resolution 58/126 of 19 December 2003 for election of the main committee chairs.

35 GA Resolution 57/301 of 13 March 2002.

36 Burton, *Assembly of the League*, 110, describes League practice.

37 Under Secretary-General Stavropoulos in A/AC.149/SR.5 (30 March 1971), par. 59.

38 Michael Byers, "Agreeing to disagree: Security Council resolution 1441 and intentional ambiguity," *Global Governance* 10(2): 165–86 (2004).

39 The number and variety of informal discussions is indicated by the meeting listings in the *Journal of the United Nations* for 6 July 2004 during the resumed 58th session.

40 E.g. the Second Committee in UN Doc. A/C.2/58//L.1 (23 September 2003).

41 As GA Resolution 3379 (XXIX) on "Elimination of racial discrimination."

42 A/AC.149/SR.22 (7 June 1971), 136–51.

43 GA Resolution S-10/2, par. 117 of 30 June 1978.

44 C.V. Narasimhan, *The United Nations: An Insider's View* (New Delhi: 1988), 60, recalls it as "overwhelmingly female" in the 1960s and 1970s. The assembly's two woman presidents, India's Vijaya Lakshmi Pandit (9th session, 1954) and Liberia's Angie Brooks (24th session, 1969), were among the few exceptions to this pattern in their days.

45 Erskine Childers and Brian Uruquart, "Renewing the UN system," *Development Dialogue* 1994/1, 128, report that the Third Committee was 30 percent female and the other committees anywhere from 8 percent to 17 percent female in 1991.

46 Report of the Special Committee on the Rationalization of the Procedures and Organization of the General Assembly, UN Doc. A/8426 (September 1971), par 110–17.

47 In 2003 the Fourth Committee allocated five of its 24 meetings to colonial items. See plan of work in UN Doc. A/58/C.4/L1 of 26 September 2003.

48 GA Resolution 2625 (XXV) of 24 October 1970.

49 Resolution 3043 (XXVII) of 19 December 1972.

50 GA Decisions 38/32 of 25 November 1983 and 38/429 of 19 December 1983.

51 Resolutions 48/87 of16 December 1993 and 49/85 of 15 December 1994 formalized this trend.

52 See, for example, the debate about whether to substitute a new draft reflecting the just-concluded Lancaster House Agreement on transition to black majority rule in Rhodesia (Zimbabwe) for the existing Fourth Committee draft A/34/PV.108, 18 December 1979.

53   The Nordic UN Project, *The United Nations in Development: Reform Issues in the Economic and Social Fields* (Stockholm: 1991), 31.

54   Resolution 377 (V) of 3 November 1950.

55   Despite objections from the Soviet bloc, which was concerned with protecting itself from the US-led majority, Resolution 377 (V) defined a council decision to transfer a matter to the assembly as a procedural question decided by a simple majority and not subject to the veto.

56   See the records of debates in UN Doc. S/PV. 751 (31 October 1956) and UN Doc. A/E-1/PV.561 (1 November 1956).

57   *UN Juridical Yearbook* 1968, 185, where it is described without comment.

58   Charles William Maynes, "The United Nations in today's world," in Toby Trister Gati (ed.), *The US, the UN, and the Management of Global Change* (New York: 1983).

59   See, for example, Commission on Global Governance, ICISS, and Secretary-General's High Level Panel on Threats, Challenges, and Change, *A More Secure World: Our Shared Responsibility* (December 2004) accessible at *www.un.org/secureworld/*.

60   A/26/Supp. 26, Doc. A/8426 (September 1971), par. 44; A/C.6/4/SR.156 (8 October 1949), par. 1–43; A/5423 (28 May 1963), par. 62.

61   GA Resolutions 58/126 of 19 December 2003 and 58/316 of 1 July 2004.

62   A/2/PV.91 (23 September 1947), 300 and A/4/PV.224 (22 September 1949), 23.

63   E.g. the USA's 1955 "open skies" proposal on mutual verification of arms control agreements, Malta's 1967 proposal to regulate resource activity beyond the edge of the continental margin, or the USSR's 1979 treaty on non-use of force.

64   As in 1960 when an emergency session began with a debate on admitting several new members before taking up the Congo situation. See UN Doc. A/E-4/PV. 858 (17 September 1960).

65   This does not prevent "tactical absence" – being in the meeting hall but not entering a response on the electronic voting machine. See Marin-Bosch, *Votes in the General Assembly*, 36. Prior to installation of the electronic vote-counting apparatus in 1966, tactical absence on roll-call votes was obvious because it required responding with the word "absent" after the country's name was called.

66   The first three by rules 87 and 126; the fourth by an understanding noted in A/18/PV.1266 (6 November 1963), par. 19–20.

67   Agreement to carry over this practice from the League Assembly noted in A/1/C.1/PV.13 (5 November 1946), 43–6; formal specification appeared in the 1947 version of assembly rules of procedure (UN Doc. A/250 (December 1947)). League practice discussed in Burton, *Assembly of the League,* 19–20.

68   E.g. Marin-Bosch, *Voting in the General Assembly*, 29.

69   Remarks of French, Czech, Hungarian, and Romanian delegates in A/AC.121/SR.1 (22 April 1965), 4. Assembly definition of "unanimous vote" discussed in A/14/PV.846 (5 December 1959), par. 37–41, 96–9, 163–4, and 167.

70   Herve Cassin, "Le consensus dans la pratique des Nations Unis," *Annuaire Française de droit international* 1977, 456–85.

71   Report of the Special Committee on the Rationalization of the Procedures and Organization of the General Assembly, UN Doc. A/8426 (September 1971), par. 289.

72   Marie-Claude Smouts, "The General Assembly: grandeur and decadence," in Paul Taylor and A.J.R. Groom (eds), *The United Nations at the Millennium: The Principal Organs* (London and New York: 2000), 31. Even the UN Secretariat seems unsure of its significance because it notes whether a resolution is adopted "by consensus"

or "without a vote" in individual meeting records and the annual *UN Yearbook* summaries, but not in the annual compilation of General Assembly resolutions.

73 This aspect of the assembly is emphasized by close observers like Conor Cruise O'Brien, *The United Nations: Sacred Drama* (New York: 1968), or Hernane Tavares de Sa, *The Play within the Play: The Inside Story of the United Nations* (New York: 1966).

74 A/15/PV.877, par. 130 (29 September 1960).

75 In folk memory, he had a pistol in the holster. Brian Urquhart insists in *A Life in Peace and War* (New York: 1987), 261, that the holster was empty but says news photographs did not reveal that detail.

76 UN Doc. A/15/PV.

77 UN Doc. A/26/PV.

78 A/51/PV.

79 A/57PV.

80 See Allen Hovey, Jnr, "Obstructionism and the rules of the General Assembly," *International Organization* 5: 515–30 (1951), and Siegfried E.Werners, *The Presiding Officers in the United Nations* (Haarlem, Netherlands: 1967), 151–2.

81 UN Doc. A/8426 (September 1971), par. 146–7 and GA Resolution 57/301 (13 March 2002).

82 A/AC.149/SR.14 (17 May 1971), 27.

83 January 1983 conversation with Oscar Schachter, a member of the Secretariat from 1944 through 1976.

The General Assembly, the
member states, and the rest
of the UN system

When delegates in the General Assembly adopt resolutions and decisions they
are asking others to conduct themselves in particular ways. Most often these
addressees are member states or elements of the UN system, but sometimes
they are other intergovernmental organizations, international, national, or local
NGOs, business firms or individuals. Since the assembly has no administrative
machinery and lacks the resources to create material incentives or disincentives,
its resolutions and decisions affect world politics only if enough of the
addressees decide for their own reasons to act as the assembly suggests. It can be
hard to trace the effect of assembly resolutions on NGOs, firms, and individuals
because their relation is so distant. Much closer are the connections between the
assembly and UN member states or other UN bodies. Examining how assembly
resolutions affect their choices and conduct permits elucidating the major part
of the General Assembly's political significance.

The General Assembly and the member states

UN member states are the most significant addressees of assembly resolutions
because governments possess most of the capabilities needed for implementing
them. Unlike the League of Nations, the UN has always included all of the
great powers,[1] and today counts nearly all states in the world among its
members. Thus it appears to have greater potential for influencing world politics than did the League Assembly. Like it, however, the General Assembly does
not have the same influence as a legislature in a national system. Much of the
assembly's influence arises more indirectly, through organizational decisions or
influence on domestic-level political actors.

Direct influence on member states

Article 10 of the Charter specifies that most assembly resolutions and decisions
are recommendations. Despite the scattered arguments among international

lawyers that the General Assembly has acquired some legislative or quasi-legislative authority over member states noted in Chapter 1, governments continue to regard assembly resolutions as recommendations to be followed or ignored as they chose. They can, and occasionally have, specified at the time of adoption that they regard the terms of a particular resolution as expressing legal obligations.[2]

States generally prefer settling their disputes through direct negotiations or with help from a mediator. Only when those procedures fail do they begin to consider other modes of settlement. On a few occasions, mostly early in the UN's history, pairs or groups of member states have agreed in advance that they would submit a dispute to the assembly and accept its suggestions on settlement as binding.[3] Yet this has not been a prominent part of assembly activity for several reasons. First, states can choose among a large number of procedures for particular disputes, such as arbitration, WTO dispute settlement panels, or applying peer pressure through environmental regime implementation committees. Both of the Cold War blocs preferred, and Third World government still prefer, dealing with intra-bloc or intra-regional political disputes among themselves. On most occasions, when a political dispute is brought to the assembly, one side is more eager for assembly involvement than the other, and the estimates of majority senti-ment influencing each side's attitude are apparent to all. While the side confident of majority support will be happy to accept the assembly's sugges-tions as binding determinations, the side anticipating an unfriendly audience will avoid any such commitment. This does not prevent assembly majorities from making suggestions or taking sides, but does mean it seldom serves as a third-party decision-maker.

Influence based on power to create administrative facts

Though unable to command states, the assembly can create some facts that states cannot ignore through its organizational decisions. The impact of such decisions on states is most direct in two areas: 1) designation of the states or other entities entitled to participate in assembly and assembly-sponsored activity, and of who will be accepted as their representatives, and 2) approval of the UN budget and apportionment of assessments among the member states.[4] The assembly exerts less direct effect through its authority to create its own subsidiary bodies, an influence that will be assessed later.

The General Assembly shares authority to endorse claims to statehood by admitting a territorial entity to UN membership. While the assembly could reject a Security Council recommendation, in practice the Security Council has been the main focus of debate over applicants' eligibility because decisions about membership are subject to the veto and the General Assembly cannot act without a prior recommendation from the Security Council.[5] Majority coalitions further eclipsed the assembly's role in the 1940s by endorsing the principle of universal membership[6] and in the 1960s by urging the Security Council to accept that neither tiny territory nor small population should bar any state from membership.

However the assembly can and does indicate whether particular applicants would or would not be welcome even before the Security Council acts. The Declaration on the Granting of Independence to Colonial Countries and Peoples[7] made clear that all territories currently ruled by an extra-regional state that succeeded in negotiating or fighting for independence would be welcome. Assembly majorities emphasized this point by extending observer status to national liberation movements recognized by the Organization of African Unity and the Arab League. Conversely, assembly condemnations of the white minority Ian Smith regime in Rhodesia and the South African government's efforts to reinforce apartheid by creating "independent" black states ("Bantustans") within South Africa made clear that those entities would not be welcome.

Acting alone, the General Assembly can determine who should be accepted as the government of a particular member state whenever two or more factions claim that status. Most often, such discussions are triggered by the appearance in New York of rival delegations seeking accreditation as delegates of the same member state. The assembly, either in plenary discussion or by turning the question over to the Credentials Committee, can influence the factions' relative international standing by choosing one or ignoring all.

The longest controversy ran from 1950 and 1971, when most assembly sessions included debate over whether delegates from the Republic of China (ROC, based in Taipei) or from the People's Republic of China (PRC, based in Beijing) should be seated as representatives of China. By traditional rules for recognition of governments, which emphasize effective control, the PRC claim was far stronger by late 1949. However, the Korean War and other events inspired the US-led majority to use its voting power and various procedural maneuvers to maintain the ROC delegates in place until September 1971.[8] Then and since, the PRC government has maintained majority support for excluding the ROC even from observer status.[9] The assembly also had to choose between rival delegations when two delegations arrived from the Republic of the Congo (later Zaire) in 1960 and when two arrived from Yemen in 1962. The tangled post-Khmer Rouge politics of Cambodia triggered the longest of three arguments about Cambodian delegations in 1979.[10] Few were sorry to see the Khmer Rouge overthrown in December 1978. However, the fact this was accomplished by Vietnamese intervention led a majority to continue seating delegates from an opposition coalition including the Khmer Rouge until conclusion of the 1991 Paris Accord setting in motion a process of establishing a new government under supervision of a UN transitional administration.

Factions often seek assembly acceptance because they believe this will accord them greater international standing, and perhaps some advantage at home. However, the assembly as a whole most often defers to the regional group of the affected state, so it is often regional opinion that matters more. How much assembly acceptance matters depends on the particular internal conflict. For a coherent faction clearly ruling an important state, like the PRC government, it does not matter very much.

General Assembly majorities sometimes comment on or try to influence political struggles within a country even when only one delegation arrives in New York. Between November 1956 and 1962, the US-led majority expressed disapproval of Soviet suppression of the Hungarian uprising by "taking no action" on the Hungarian delegation's credentials. Yet it also minimized the practical effect by having the Credentials Committee report at the end of the session, which allowed the Hungarian delegates to be "seated provisionally" and participate fully in the session as outlined in assembly rule 29. The Hungarians ultimately sought assistance form the UN Legal Counsel, whose advice that Hungarian credentials were in order led to discontinuing the challenge.[11]

African delegations adopted a similar tactic against the South African delegation starting in 1965. In 1973, the Third World majority increased the disapproval by "rejecting" their credentials.[12] That year's president, Leopoldo Benites of Ecuador, did not regard this decision as barring the South African delegates from the assembly. However, the following year's president, Abdelaziz Bouteflika of Algeria, interpreted an identical decision as barring them and a Western motion to reverse the ruling was defeated by a vote of 91 to 22 with 19 abstentions.[13] South African efforts to challenge the exclusion were turned back at the 34th session in 1979 and the eighth emergency session (on Namibia) in March 1981. Not until 1994 after the apartheid regime was replaced were South African delegates again seated in the assembly.

The Arab group appeared ready to make a similar challenge to Israeli credentials at the 37th session in response to Israel's June 1982 invasion of Lebanon. Strong US warnings and moderate Arab states' own sense that it would be a bad move at a moment when an Arab summit had just endorsed the latest US peace proposals and everyone was waiting for an Israeli response to them meant it did not arise.[14] More recently, the assembly acted in tandem with the Security Council when it barred delegates from the Federal Republic of Yugoslavia from participating in 1992. This followed a Security Council determination that the FRY was not a continuation of the prior Socialist

Federal Republic of Yugoslavia and should apply for UN membership like the other former Yugoslav republics.[15]

General Assembly decisions about observer status and seating of delegations have direct effect only within the assembly and its subordinate bodies. While the Security Council follows assembly determinations regarding delegations, other United Nations bodies make their own decisions. These may parallel those of the assembly, or may take rejection even further, depending on what a majority of their member states will accept. In the end, political survival as a government depends partly on international opinion but even more on ability to prevail at the domestic level. Representation internationally helps with the former, but cannot make up for inability to prevail at home.

On a literal reading of Charter Article 17, the General Assembly can commit member states to paying for whatever UN activities it establishes:

1) The General Assembly shall consider and approved the budget of the organization.
2) The expenses of the organization shall be borne by the members as apportioned by the General Assembly.

In practice, member states have succeeded in limiting their exposure by keeping the budget relatively small, denying the UN authority to tax nonstate entities, and keeping it on a tight financial leash through laggard payment of assessments.

Both aspects of the budget, determining how much to allocate to various UN activities and the size of each member states' contribution toward the budget, have been subjects of constant controversy. Much of it stems from the disjuncture between shares of budget assessment and shares of assembly voting power. In a highly unequal international system, it is not surprising that assessments based on economic size will not match up with votes distributed on a one state–one vote rule. How the disjuncture plays out in the assembly's budget and assessment decisions depends very much on the pattern of coalitions.

Assessments are based first on "ability to pay" – calculated on formulas using both per capita income and national share of world production – but this principle has been qualified in several ways. First, some of the poorer members – initially states that had suffered severe devastation during the Second World War, and later developing countries – were assessed at rates lower than their underlying ability to pay. This often meant paying the minimum assessment – 0.04 percent in 1946, 0.02 percent after 1972, and 0.01 percent after 1977 (with the tiniest states assessed at 0.001 percent after 1997). Second, the USA has been assessed at a rate lower than suggested by its share of world gross product: at 38.89 percent in 1946, 33.33 percent in 1954, 25 percent in 1972, and 22 percent since 2000.[16] Together, the "ceiling" and "floor" placed a greater than proportional burden on the Western European states and Japan. Until 1974 these countries had an implicit ceiling in the form of an understanding that they should not pay more per capita than the USA. All countries also benefited from rules avoiding sudden large changes in assessment by calculating them on a three- to six-year rolling average of national economic performance.

Peacekeeping operations have been financed through separate accounts, which since 1973 have used a different scale. In the initial version,[17] the least developed countries paid 10 percent of their regular budget contribution rate (0.002 percent until 1977 and 0.001 percent thereafter), other developing countries paid 20 percent of their regular assessments, industrial countries paid the same portion as their regular assessment, and the Permanent 5 paid more to make up the difference. This typically put US peacekeeping assessments 5–6 percent above its regular budget share.

Though, as many member governments like to put it, assessments should be paid 'in full, on time, and without conditions,'[18] the assembly has little ability to enforce the assessments. This weakness shows up most immediately in widespread late payment. Though assessments are due in January, many member states pay much later in the year. The USA gets the most publicity since it accounts for such a large share of the late payments, still withholds sums that would go to certain programs, and because the executive branch has made clear that it will pay only after Congress adopts the budget in October. However, it is not the only laggard in the group. In 2000, a fairly typical year, only 43 of the then 189 member states had paid their full assessments by the end of January, and only 117 of them were fully paid up by the end of December.[19] Persistent slow payment forces the Secretariat into a variety of expedients for keeping the organization running as the money trickles in. Some Specialized Agencies – ITU, UPU, and ICAO – can charge interest for late payments, but member states have not given similar authority to the General Assembly.

With members going beyond slow payment to withholding of contributions, an assembly majority's first resource is peer pressure, but this makes little impression on recalcitrant nonpayers. Its only other resource is Article 19 of the Charter, which specifies that:

> A Member of the United Nations which is in arrears in the payment of its financial contributions to the Organization shall have no vote in the General Assembly if the amount equals or exceeds the amount of the contributions due from it for the preceding two years. The General Assembly may, nevertheless, permit such a Member to vote if it is

satisfied that the failure to pay is due to conditions beyond the control of the Member.

Loss of voting rights does not keep a delegation from participating in assembly meetings, and is less obvious when the assembly is operating by consensus, but most governments do not like the public embarrassment of getting so far behind in contributions that Article 19 might be applied to them.

Until the early 1960s, arguments about the size and uses of the UN budget were largely East–West disagreements about particular activities. The Soviet bloc, conscious of its minority position, worried about US-led attempts to use the UN for Cold War purposes. The Soviet bloc therefore sought to keep the budget as small as possible and also to minimize what it would have to pay for UN activities it viewed as most directly serving Western interests, such as the Korean Operation and UNEF I. It was able to win agreement in 1956 that peacekeeping operations would be run through separate accounts, preparing the way for arguments about whether peacekeeping was or was not part of the "regular budget" covered by Article 19. The Soviet bloc also supported decisions to finance much of UN development activity through separate voluntary funds. This frustrated Third World efforts to get such programs included in the regular budget, but meant that the Soviets would not have to pay for what they regarded as undoing the harm done to Third World countries by colonialism and capitalism. Thus there was much truth to British Prime Minister Macmillan's 1961 comment that at the UN "there is the compulsory subscription and the voluntary subscription. The only difference between them is this. The compulsory is the one that you do not pay if you do not want to, and the voluntary is the one that you need not pay unless you wish to."[20]

Arguments over peacekeeping assessments intensified in the early 1960s as the UN Operation in the Congo ran up massive bills because of the need to prevent secession by mineral-rich Katanga Province and to mediate fierce political competition between factions led by President Kasavubu and Prime Minister Lumumba. Politics within the assembly heated up as the Western powers and much of the Third World supported Kasavubu while the Soviet bloc and more radical Third World states supported Lumumba. As costs continued to mount and they became more dissatisfied with it, the Soviet Union, France, and some other members began refusing to pay their assessments for the Congo operation.

In September 1964 the Soviet Union and France were close to two years behind on their assessments, and Article 19 on everyone's mind. Although the US government initially took the position that the peacekeeping accounts were part of the regular budget covered by Article 19, it backed off in the face of majority unwillingness to confront the USSR and France. The essence of the French and Soviet positions was captured by a Latin American observer of UN affairs in a fictional dialogue between two delegates. The Scandinavian, recalling that neither the Soviets nor the French had vetoed the Suez or Congo operations, asks "why shouldn't they pay if they consented?" The Latin American replies:

> You are confusing consent with tolerance. I have a son who stays out late almost every evening. I don't like it but I don't try to stop him. ... But every so often he tries to borrow my car and every time I refuse. I tolerate his staying out late, but I won't go as far as actively subsidizing it by providing transportation.[21]

The experience reinforced the idea that member states cannot be forced to pay, a theme sounded very clearly in a US statement that paved the way for returning to normal assembly routines without applying Article 19. As US ambassador Goldberg put it, "we must make it crystal clear that if any member can insist on making an exception to the principle of collective financial responsibility with respect to certain activities of the Organization, the United States reserves the same option to make exceptions if, in our view, strong and compelling reasons exist for doing so."[22] The impacts were noticed most immediately in security issues, where the experience left the membership uninterested in large UN peacekeeping operations and reinforced the separation between the "regular" and the "peacekeeping" budgets.

Even at the lower totals of the 1970s, arguments about the size of the regular budget and the uses of funds continued as the Third World majority pressed for a significant increase in financing of development activities. These had begun in 1949 with an Expanded Program of Technical Assistance, supplemented in 1958 by a Special UN Fund for Development. Though operated by the UN Development Programme (UNDP) after 1965, neither was as large as developing states wished. Pressure to increase UN development funding attained considerable success in the mid to late 1970s, with the UN budget increasing from approximately $400 million in 1970 to approximately $2,000 million in 1982. Even with rejection of their most ambitious proposals, the Third World was securing increases at a pace greatly exceeding the rate of global inflation at the time. Some Western governments grumbled, but none was prepared at that point to challenge the decisions.

The next round of contention over assessments arose in the late 1970s as the impact of the 1973 oil price increases started to be reflected in the rolling averages of national economic performance. With abolition of the per capita limit in 1974, OPEC members and a few other states faced significant increases in assessments that they sought to limit. At the same time, countries suffering severe balance of payments deficits because of the oil price increases wanted to avoid being stuck with higher assessments themselves because of any relief given to OPEC members. Only after very hard internal bargaining did the Group of 77 agree to a new assessment formula in 1977. OPEC members won some delay in increases when the assessment formula was shifted from a three-year to a seven-year rolling average. The poorest countries got the minimum assessment reduced to 0.01 percent, and more populous developing countries like India and Indonesia were able to shift some of the burden to less populous oil-rich counterparts like Kuwait and Brunei by adjusting the per capita component of the assessment formula. Meanwhile China used its influence to get its assessment reduced from the 5 percent that the ROC had accepted in 1946, a figure then and later much higher than China's share of world production, to 0.88 percent.

The increased assessments laid on Western and Soviet bloc states under the 1977 formula would not have caused as much unhappiness if the regular budget had not continued to grow and Third World contributions had not shrunk further in the debt crisis of the 1980s. While the 117 Third World members together paid 11.73 percent of the budget under the 1977 assessments, their collective share dropped to 9.86 percent in the scale for 1983. The Soviets complained that this meant shifting another $68.5 million worth of the budget on to other members. US commentary was even more hostile, particularly after the assembly's 1981 budget resolutions increased the regular budget by 12 percent at a moment when global inflation was 1–2 percent.[23]

In response, both the Reagan administration and the US Congress began pressing for change. The former sought "zero growth" budgets (increases no more than the rate of inflation), withheld payments for some activities, and transferred the rest even later than usual. In 1986 Congress specified that it would not authorize paying more than 20 percent of the regular UN budget unless and until the rest of the membership agreed to make budget decisions under a rule weighting votes by size of assessment. The Third World majority reacted angrily, with delegations saying it "detracted from" or "subverted" the UN's basic democratic principles.[24] However, both sides backed off as other governments perceived that the Reagan administration would accept a compromise under which budget decisions would be made by consensus following a new procedure giving the "major contributors" a greater role in the budget-drafting process. This was accomplished by giving the Committee for Programme and Co-ordination, which had been created to help the Economic and Social Council co-ordinate UN programs, the task of advising the Fifth Committee on budgets and enlarging it from 21 to 34 members to include more of the major contributors.

The vast increase in conflict resolution and peacekeeping activity inspired significant increases in the UN budget in the early 1990s, and a new round of contention. This began in 1995 when the Republican-controlled US Congress began insisting that US peacekeeping contributions should be capped at 25 percent. The Democratic Clinton administration, though more supportive of the UN, offered no significant opposition. Members of the EU objected to the unilateralism of the US move, but had already concluded that the peace-keeping formula needed revision in light of recent economic changes. The assessment issue moved to the forefront of assembly attention in 1999 after the US Congress expanded its demands by mandating that the USA pay no more than 22 percent of the regular budget (instead of 25 percent) and no more than 25 percent of the peacekeeping budget (instead of 31 percent). Discussions took their usual form of working out a formula that would look evenhanded at first glance but include details shifting the burden in particular ways. Tough and complex negotiations ensued during the Assembly's 2000 session.[25] US negotiators sought the Congressionally-mandated reductions, other industrial states sought to limit increases in their assessments, newly industrializing and "middle-income" developing states strove both to limit the size and defer the effective date of increases in their contributions, and low-income countries sought to keep their contributions at previous levels. The net result gave the USA most of what it wanted (its peacekeeping assessment remained above 25 percent) and produced a 10-category formula for peacekeeping contributions that distinguished more clearly among Third World countries by their economic performance. Newly industrializing and middle-income countries like South Korea, Singapore, Qatar, Kuwait, India, and Brazil now had to take up more of the burden.[26] On the regular budget side, increases in assessments of the more prosperous Third World countries had brought the Third World's collective share of payments back almost to the 11.73 percent they had paid in 1977.[27] Considering the economic growth of some developing countries in the mean time, the result indicates considerable Third World success in keeping the burdens on the industrial countries.

Two developments, the greater distinctions among developing countries in the assessment scales, and the experiences of developing country delegates serving on the CPC with shaping and then explaining to the rest of the G-77 the budget decisions being proposed, appear likely to alter UN budget dynamics. They will not affect the domestic sources of US budget positions, but do mean that those positions get presented in a different international milieu than existed in the early 1980s. As collective unhappiness with the Iraq War wanes or is over-lain by other issues, the split of the Third World coalition into "ideologue" and "pragmatist" wings[28] will also affect bargaining dynamic.

The UN remains heavily dependent on a relatively small portion of its membership for funds. In 2002, two member states – the USA and Japan – paid about 41.51 percent of the assessments, the EU 15 paid another 36.84 percent, and five other industrial states paid 6.35 percent. Almost half (7.73

percent) of the remaining 15.30 percent was supplied by five countries. The last 7.93 percent was provided by 163 members, more than enough to form a two-thirds majority. The divergence between votes and resources that led to industrial state insistence on consensus budget-making will not weaken any time soon.

Influence over the normative context in which states operate

Control over the trends in international events is exercised by states and other actors rather than by the General Assembly. However, the assembly can influence the development of international norms, and hence the broader milieu within which states and other actors operate, by endorsing or condemning particular types of activity or particular practices. This function of collective legitimization is the assembly's most significant contribution to the direction of world politics. Assembly resolutions suggesting general principles or rules of conduct to the member states provide the most general normative influence, while its comments on particular issues or disputes help round out the general statements. The assembly also exerts influence on the direction of normative discussion by sponsoring diplomatic conferences that draft global multilateral treaties on particular subjects or convening global conferences or summits to address particular issues.

Resolutions formulating general norms may be urging states to adopt new norms, as in the Universal Declaration of Human Rights,[29] or may be reminding them of previously-established ones, as in the Declaration on the Inadmissibility of Intervention into the Domestic Affairs of States.[30] These resolutions usually follow lengthy consideration and are highlighted by using the word "declaration" in their title.

The assembly differs from national legislatures in lacking ways to provide addressees with positive or negative incentives to heed its words. A national legislature can link its words to punishments or inducements by incorporating them into the national legal system and relying on executive branch agencies to reward compliance or punish noncompliance by the various natural persons and legal persons in the country. The General Assembly must rely on the persuasive power of its words, so the impacts these general declarations depends on how well the desires of the assembly majority adopting them match up with the desires of significant actors in the broader international system.

Well-established norms and rules have several political effects. At the very least, they pressure governments into explaining nonconforming conduct to other governments, and sometimes to their own and other countries' citizens. Widespread support for the Charter prohibition against first use of armed force means governments try even harder now than in the nineteenth or early twentieth centuries to explain how their proposed use of force is consistent with the Charter. Governments sensitive to outside opinion may well alter policy rather than face criticism, but governments not particularly sensitive to it may become more set in their choice. This can be seen in the varying responses to pressures for decolonization. The Charter and assembly resolutions reinforced domestic critics of empire in Britain and France, and helped make the process of winding down those empires more peaceful that it would have been. Yet those same criticisms of colonial policy had no effect on the Portuguese government; decolonization began only after a military coup in 1974 established a new government ready to concede the colonies' independence.

Governments and other actors conforming to widely shared norms and rules can easily defend their conduct by pointing to the norm or rule. General Assembly resolutions that enjoy wide and persistent support thus become part of the evidence that the norm is widely shared, and items to be mentioned in defense of conforming conduct. Conversely, governments violating a widely shared norm or rule will need to show either that it is irrelevant to the particular situation or that their conduct conforms to an equally important or more important norm. However, power calculations are seldom far from the surface in states' choices of conduct; the international community of states is small enough that who is acting can matter as much as what is done. The lack of linkage with a wider rivalry helps explain why Tanzanian government faced little criticism for overthrowing the Idi Amin government of Uganda in mid-1978 while the Vietnamese faced considerable criticism for overthrowing the Khmer Rouge government of Cambodia a few months later because of perceptions its action was part of a wider Sino-Soviet competition.

Controversial norms and rules, no matter how often restated by the assembly, will not elicit much compliance. Defying weakly shared norms may even help a government increase its domestic support if important groups within the country also question or oppose the norm. Governments disinclined to obey a controversial norm or rule can simply ignore it, proceeding as if it does not exist and using political rather than legal arguments to justify noncompliance.

General Assembly majorities can also try to affect the discourse of world politics by using resolutions to set out theories of causation – that is, make statements about why some particular condition arises or persists. These statements attribute blame or credit for some outcome to certain circumstances or (more often) to certain actors. When the outcome is undesirable, assembly majorities are suggesting that altering those circumstances or changing the conduct of those actors will improve the situation. Thus, in the 1970s and 1980s the Third World majority adopted a long string of resolutions claiming that the activities of "foreign economic interests" (multinational corporations) were inhibiting decolonization and the elimination of racist regimes in southern Africa. Similarly, a long string of resolutions on international economic questions rested on Marxist and other structuralist arguments attributing the poverty of developing states entirely to the workings of the global capitalist system. Governments rejecting this statement of cause worked hard to get it removed or toned down, with relatively little success before 1991.

A theory of causation that focuses too narrowly or suffers empirical disconfirmation cannot support a General Assembly majority in the long run. As superpower tensions abated in the mid-1950s, the US government came to realize that focusing only on political-strategic competition between the blocs was not particularly appealing to Third World governments more concerned about ending colonialism and promoting economic development. By the early 1980s even the Soviets were losing confidence that government planning and de-linking from the global economy were recipes for success in economic development, a sentiment strengthened later in the decade by contrasting Latin American and East Asian economic performance. The intellectual basis of the radical hold over the Nonaligned began to erode, producing a much more complex dynamic of coalition-maintenance.

Influence through bureaucratic uptake

Compliance with assembly suggestions is enhanced when they are incorporated into the standard operating procedures of government agencies because this makes compliance the "default mode" of action. Incorporation may be explicit, such as incorporation of a resolution's language into domestic law or administrative regulations, or it may be tacit, with a particular agency adopting the international standard on its own. Many assembly statements are too vague to be used in this way; they seek to provide broad policy guidance for governments rather than instructions for implementing agencies. However, some are specific enough to serve as benchmarks. Resolutions recommending trade sanctions suggest very specific agency responses (do not issue export licenses, do not provide export credits, do not allow certain goods through customs checks). The often-repeated statement that industrial states should devote a sum equivalent to 0.7 percent of their national product to aid for developing countries guides budgeting in some industrial countries and provides a yardstick to intergovernmental organizations, NGOs, and citizens interested in comparing their foreign policies. Similarly, even with widespread agreement that few of them will be met within the original time-frame, the Millennium Development Goals have focused assessments of development efforts more clearly on the conditions of the poorest than previous statements of development goals.

Influence in particular conflicts

General norms or rules can be applied in a particular conflict to distinguish between actors whose positions deserve support from those whose positions deserve opposition. However, assembly majorities can, and often do, go further and adopt resolutions dealing specifically with a particular conflict or dispute. It might proceed evenhandedly, calling on both sides to settle the conflict peacefully and reminding them in general terms of relevant international norms, or it might take sides by endorsing one side's position or criticizing another's. Resolutions taking sides vary in intensity, ranging from mild preferences for or against one side to unqualified endorsement or condemnation.

For many years, the government of South Africa was the target of unrelenting criticism and of statements that its very existence was illegitimate phrased with an intensity that was often a substitute for action. No member state supported the apartheid policy, but the major Western powers were not prepared to overthrow a government that they regarded as a barrier to the spread of communism in its part the world. Allowing the assembly to condemn South Africa and ostracize it from the UN became a substitute for serious action against apartheid[31] until a combination of increasing domestic pressure and waning Soviet challenge cleared the way for some action in the 1990s.

All-out verbal engagement favoring one side then spread to the Arab–Israeli/Israeli–Palestinian conflict. North African states, particularly Algeria, belonging to both the African and Arab groups encouraged each to support and reinforce the demands of the other. Thus the Arab group supported the sub-Saharan African states' position on South Africa, and received considerable African support for anti-Israel campaigns. Even with the end of the apartheid regime, much of this coalition continues to hold on the Israeli–Palestinian conflict. Though the 1975 declaration that "Zionism is a form of racism"[32] was formally repealed in 1991,[33] Israel continues to be the subject of intense condemnation by the assembly.

As outsiders easy to condemn, apartheid South Africa and Israel helped maintain the increasingly fragile Third World coalition by providing a common rallying point. Stable assembly coalitions usually avoid condemning states in good standing with significant elements of the coalition. Reformists and the legally minded often deplore the resulting "double standards," but the maxim "protect your friends and punish your enemies" always operates in political arenas. The end of the Cold War merely altered the mode of its application by removing the simple right–left litmus tests applied by both superpower blocs.

Whether declaring general norms or commenting on specific conflicts, General Assembly resolutions are exercises in symbolic politics. Their impact depends very much on the relation between ability to control the issuance of symbolic statements and ability to create outcomes through political inter-action. Thus their impact depends heavily on the way in which the goals of the assembly majority align with the material capability of the states most able to create actual outcomes in the international system.

The logical possibilities can be summarized in the 2-by-2 matrix shown in Figure 4.1.

A coalition of strong states seeking minor change or preservation of the status quo cannot ignore symbolic politics, though need not rely heavily on it. Even that sort of coalition needs arguments that will encourage its own members to act consistently with coalition goals and provide a basis for defending those goals against criticism by others. Modest goals need not mean employing subdued rhetoric, particularly in contentions with coalitions seeking major changes. Faced with the ideological challenges of the Soviet bloc, the US-led majority used the assembly to defend its vision of the world and vigorously challenge the competing Soviet vision.

The Soviet bloc was a good example of a coalition with significant (though not overwhelming) material capability desiring major changes in the interna-tional system. As a coalition with a highly articulated ideology, it used symbolic politics extensively; however, its small numbers in the General Assembly meant that it had to rely more on debate and submission of proposals than on securing adoption of its ideas. Coalescence of the Nonaligned around a solidly left-wing leadership in the 1970s gave the Soviet bloc more opportunities in the assembly. However, skepticism of multilateral institutions dominated by nonsocialist states meant that the Soviet bloc usually preferred to apply its ample resources to political efforts outside the assembly.

Whatever their goals, coalitions possessing little material capability face a very different situation. Such a coalition must guard against being victimized by coalitions wielding considerable material capability on behalf of incompat-ible goals while seeking allies who will help advance its own goals. The General Assembly provides little protection against victimization; it is at most a place where the weak can try to influence the strong's actions by invoking shared principles and norms. It also provides opportunities for recruiting allies through persuasion. Such efforts can take any or all of three forms. First, the weak coalition may try to show stronger states how their own beliefs, logically and consistently applied, entail acceptance of the weak coali-tion's goals. Hence the heavy Third World reliance on such abstract but widely accepted concepts as equity, self-determination, and nondiscrimina-tion. Second, the weak coalition may try to demonstrate to stronger states that accepting the goals is consistent with their own self-interest. The Group of 77 largely avoided this sort of argument on economic development in the

Figure 4.1 Resolution Impact Matrix

		Goal	
		Major change	Minor change or status quo
	Strong	a	b
Capability			
	Weak	c	d

1970s and 1980s; intellectuals and others in the West often had to make it themselves. Third, the weak can try to appeal to emotions that will carry the strong in the desired direction. In the 1970s and 1980s the Third World coalition did try to play on Western feelings of guilt about the legacies of colonialism. Such arguments had considerable influence in the more left-wing segments of Western public opinion. Certain Western governments – most notably the Scandinavians and the Dutch – exhibited strong sympathy with Third World aspirations. However, the guilt rhetoric had little effect on the major Western powers or Japan and proved insufficient to secure acceptance of the most expansive visions of a new international economic order.

How heavily a coalition of the weak employs symbolic politics depends on whether it is seeking major change or is largely content with the status quo. Efforts to secure major changes require more persuasion and hence greater use of symbolic politics unless the weak find (as they thought they had in the OPEC price increases) some material leverage over the strong. As disappointments piled up in the 1970s, the Third World majority's internal dynamics further encouraged bold claims and strident rhetoric on the key economic issues as ways to maintain the coalition by presenting the sum of all members' demands. The Third World coalition remains heavily reliant on symbolic politics but its goals have changed. Most members accept reliance on markets as the "only economic policy game in town" but want to combine that reliance with more government regulation and supervision than preferred by the sort of economic neoliberals more accurately described as "free market fundamentalists."

The General Assembly and the Security Council

The Charter establishes the General Assembly and the Security Council as "principal organs" of the United Nations, but member governments have always regarded the Security Council as "the aristocracy" and the General

Assembly as "the masses."[34] The Charter provisions defining their areas of concern and authority *vis-à-vis* member states give each a distinct position within the United Nations system. The Security Council, consisting of five permanent and ten elected members, has authority to instruct members in making a collective response to a threat to the peace, a breach of the peace, or an act of aggression. However, it can only exercise that authority when nine members agree and all five permanent members either vote yes or abstain. A no vote from any one of the permanent members, or from seven of the elected members, prevents application of collective measures. Besides providing a general forum where members can raise any security-related concern, the General Assembly can also serve as either an alternate route to collective action or as a parallel forum where the rest of the membership can comment on the Security Council's handling of a particular crisis.

Alternate route to UN action

While several of the smaller member states protested against inclusion of veto powers in the Charter, it was the US-led majority that pioneered the idea of using the General Assembly to bypass a stalemated Security Council. Building on provisions in Charter Articles 10 and 12 that permit the General Assembly to discuss conflicts that might lead to war and to adopt resolutions regarding those conflicts if the Security Council is not acting, the US-led majority created the "Uniting for Peace" process for calling the assembly into emergency session and having it, rather than the Security Council, take the lead in addressing some conflict or crisis.[35] The resolution let the US-led coalition maintain the UN operation in Korea after the Soviet Union had returned to the Security Council, but later permitted other states, led by India, to steer the membership toward an armistice and a compromise peace.

Though bitterly critical of the procedure and its results in 1950, the Soviets joined in invoking Uniting for Peace to bring the Suez Crisis to the assembly to avoid British and French vetoes. It was less happy about use of the General Assembly to maintain the UN operation in the Congo, but ready to use it again after the June 1967 Arab–Israeli War. In that conflict, however, the assembly ended up acting in tandem with rather than instead of the council.

An assembly majority that includes powerful states can turn the recommendations of emergency session into effective international action. An assembly majority that does not must choose between compromising sufficiently to formulate resolutions that will attract support from powerful countries and therefore be implemented, and using emergency sessions to express its own views even if those views will not attract support from powerful states. This latter path means using emergency sessions to engage in another round of symbolic politics, one that the participants hope will attract greater media and public attention through use of emergency session procedures.

Forum for the rest of the UN membership

Using emergency sessions to engage in symbolic politics points out the second aspect of the relationship between the General Assembly and the Security Council. Here, the assembly serves as a forum where the rest of the membership can comment on the proceedings and decisions of the Security Council. The Third World majority began using emergency sessions of the assembly to secure more of a say on major conflicts. The emergency sessions on Afghanistan in 1980, Palestine in 1980–2, Namibia in 1981, Israeli-occupied territory in 1982, and Israeli-occupied territory in 1997–2003 were all occasions for expressing views about a particular conflict and condemning the actions of particular parties independently of any Security Council consideration.

A combination of superpower preference for handling Cold War conflicts elsewhere and Third World governments' disinclination to air their own conflicts in the Security Council meant it was very inactive in the 1970s and 1980s. A similar pattern prevailed in the assembly, with the emergency sessions focused on only a few of the many armed conflicts underway in various parts of the world. This changed after 1987 when the USA and the Soviet Union began to use the council and council-authorized UN missions to assist in winding down a number of international or internal conflicts where they had been supporting opposite sides.

Security Council activity increased further in the early 1990s, beginning with condemnation of Iraq's invasion of Kuwait in 1991 and continuing with involvements in Somalia, reinstatement of the elected president of Haiti in 1994, and the ethnic conflicts in former Yugoslavia. All the while, the Third World majority was extremely nervous about this apparent expansion of great-power consensus to involvement in internal conflict. This nervousness was reflected in the Security Council and in the reluctance of many Third World states to approve General Assembly resolutions endorsing humanitarian intervention or suggesting that people have a right to democratic governance. Not surprisingly, European skepticism about the 2003 Iraq War found ready echo among the Third World majority; however, neither group was ready to press matters too hard lest the organization collapse.

As the council became more active, the Third World majority in the assembly realized the necessity of closer co-operation among the Third World states on the council, and between them and the rest of the majority. Mechanisms of co-operation first emerged in 1979 when Kuwaiti delegates organized a caucusing group among the Nonaligned states then serving on the Council,[36] and were strengthened in following years. By the mid-1990s Third World policy-makers and commentators were unhappy about the council's new activism, complaining that it focused only on those issues of interest to the permanent members (particularly the Western ones) and that bilateral pressures from Western countries to accept various initiatives had become very strong.[37] The council responded by initiating briefings for other delegations in 1998, more frequent meetings with delegations from states contributing troops to UN operations, and in 2004 inviting all delegations to attend and speak at "wrap up" meetings assessing Council activity in the last month or two.

The General Assembly and its own subsidiary bodies

Article 22 of the Charter permits the General Assembly to establish "such subsidiary organs as it deems necessary for the performance of its functions." This provision gives the General Assembly wide discretion to create, rearrange, or abolish a broad array of committees, expert groups, and commissions to study particular questions. The assembly is also free to change their composition, alter their size, or redefine their tasks as it chooses. In practice, the assembly favors stability in such bodies; many of them, particularly those whose missions are aligned with the preferences of a persisting assembly majority, develop a life of their own.

Standing subsidiary bodies

The long-lasting subsidiary bodies have several political effects. First, they permit the General Assembly to do more work by dividing up the tasks at hand. This effect is most obvious with a decision to create and maintain the main committees, but can also be seen in the continued existence of a range of smaller standing committees, including the Committee of 24 (Committee on Implementation of the Declaration on the Granting of Independence to Colonial Countries and Peoples) or the Committee on the Peaceful Uses of Outer Space. Unlike the main committees, these other standing committees can meet while the assembly is not in session and thereby extend its working season. Second, a standing subsidiary body affects the timing and form of international discussions on the issues it considers. The assembly's decision to create UNCTAD created a schedule of periodic meetings at which the whole membership's attention would be focused on the economic concerns of developing countries. The Third World majority saw UNCTAD as a counterweight to the trade discussions held within the conferences spun out of the General Agreement on Trade and Tariffs (GATT) dominated by the industrial states. Western industrial states regarded it as giving Third World radicals regularly scheduled occasions for proposing undesirable changes in the rules for international economic relations. UNCTAD was also the focus of a long struggle between Third World governments trying to enlarge its mandates and Western governments working to keep economic negotiations in other forums.

Third, a stable assembly majority can maintain "committed" subsidiary bodies preparing reports or draft resolutions that will channel assembly debate in predetermined ways. Bodies like the Committee of 24, the Special Committee on the Exercise of the Inalienable Rights of the Palestinian People, or the Committee against Apartheid were created by the Third World majority to express particular positions and recruit public sympathy. Because they have a continuing existence, these bodies can function even if the targets of their criticisms refuse to attend their meetings or otherwise enter into discussions with them. Only occasionally can member governments unhappy about creation of some particular subsidiary body frustrate its efforts through non-co-operation. One of the few examples occurred in 1973 when all five nuclear powers (Britain, China, France, the Soviet Union, and the USA) refused to participate in the Ad Hoc Committee on the World Disarmament Conference and all but the Soviet Union refused to participate in the Special Committee on the Distribution of Funds Released as a Result of the Reduction of Military Budgets.[38]

While created to perform tasks the majority wants done, a "committed" subsidiary body can create some problems for its creators. Such bodies tend to attract delegations with strong opinions on the question at hand, and these may not match the preferences of the majority as a whole. This skewing becomes stronger if governments that develop serious misgivings about what the body is doing drop out over time. Stable assembly majorities are reluctant to disavow the work of a subsidiary body they created, so can end up in a position where members of the majority with extreme views on the question define the goals and set the pace of debate. In the 1970s and early 1980s, a coalition of Arab and African hardliners were guiding Group of 77 positions on self-determination, apartheid, and the Arab–Israeli conflict, and often advocated positions making more moderate members of the group quite uncomfortable.

Designers of UN reform have often suggested that the assembly should reduce both the number and size of subsidiary bodies. Neither suggestion has elicited much support. Almost every subsidiary body is regarded as important by some group of delegations that will oppose its abolition. Their increasing size is a consequence of insistence that the composition of subsidiary bodies should reflect the regional composition of the General Assembly. This notion was entrenched in the late 1950s, and as the UN membership continued to grow there were periodic waves of pressure to increase the size of major subsidiary bodies to make them more "representative." By the early 1980s, with the notion of "representative" expanded to include representation for stable subregional clusters, the minimum membership stood at approximately 30. Many subsidiary bodies have become even larger owing to the conviction of many Third World delegations that participation should be open to as many delegations as possible.

Standing expert committees, such as the Committee on Contributions, have remained smaller. They typically perform specialized functions that delegations are willing to turn over to a smaller body so long as its mandate is clear and the persons who will be serving on them are chosen for their knowledge of the particular issue or task central to the mandate.

Ad hoc *treaty drafting bodies*

Though the Charter does not mention these, member governments have long used the General Assembly to organize *ad hoc* committees and conferences given the task of elaborating international rules, model national laws, or guidelines for administrative practice on some particular issue. Most often, these *ad hoc* committees and conferences report their work back to the General Assembly, which commands that work to member governments in a resolution. This process is the direct successor to the nineteenth-century practice of sponsorship by individual rulers, and provides an immediate answer to whose invitation carries sufficient prestige to attract widespread participation. Though initiating the process and endorsing it at the end, the assembly typically remains at arm's-length from it while the *ad hoc* committee or conference does its work. Yet on a major issue, such as the extensive revisions of the law of the sea negotiated between 1973 and 1982, it does comment on the proceedings and endorse particular proposals along the way.

Global conferences and summits

The notion of convening "global conferences" and "global summits" to discuss some broad issue, such as world population, the status of women, or the global environment, was a minor extension of the assembly's role as sponsor of multilateral conferences. The first global conference, on environment (Stockholm, 1972), was followed in the 1970s by conferences on food (Rome, 1974), population (Bucharest, 1974), and women (Mexico City, 1975). These conferences attracted considerable media attention because they were "special events" and typically featured organization of a parallel NGO forum at which members of relevant NGOs discussed the issues, made suggestions to the intergovernmental conference, and staged protests and other events that drew journalists. The conferences on population and women became once-a-decade events, while new conferences on environment

(Rio de Janeiro, 1992), racism (Durban, 2001), and other topics added to the stream.[39]

Each conference or summit has a distinct impact on states and other international actors; together they have come to overshadow the General Assembly. Even though the assembly typically adopts resolutions endorsing the declarations and programs of action developed at the global conferences, and some assembly special sessions provide follow-up, the declarations and programs of action remain identified with the global conference that developed them. This helps reinforce the perception that global conferences have become the most important forums for developing shared understandings of new issues and new norms for international conduct.

The General Assembly and the specialized agencies

Articles 57 and 63 of the Charter transformed the nineteenth-century "public international unions" into United Nations specialized agencies, and institutionalized the Functionalist thesis that co-operating on technical and administrative matters they could not handle alone, would lead governments to value international co-operation more highly and expand it into other areas.[40] The UN Charter put the General Assembly at one remove from this activity by specifying that the specialized agencies will all report to and have their activities co-ordinated by the Economic and Social Council. Yet it also gave the General Assembly authority to initiate studies and make recommendations about promoting international co-operation on economic, social, cultural, educational, and health questions, and in promoting respect for human rights.

The Charter's drafters expected that the assembly would be the primary forum for norm-development in these areas while an ECOSOC composed of government experts on social and economic affairs would serve as co-ordinator of operational activities. However, ECOSOC quickly became another diplomatic forum staffed by foreign service generalists and even those governments elected to it seldom used it to advance their best ideas.[41]

The elusive goal of better co-ordination

The connections among the assembly, ECOSOC, and the specialized agencies never worked as planned. Both the converted public international unions and the post-1945 creations are based on separate multilateral agreements; they also have separate memberships, budgets, and assessments on member states that give them an existence distinct from other parts of the UN system. Specialized agency rules or practices also encourage governments to send persons trained in relevant technical disciplines or employed by the relevant government agency as their delegates, which means that the specialized agencies quickly developed their own separate clienteles within governments. A wise specialized agency head carefully cultivates that clientele, both to protect his or her own position in the agency and to protect the agency from attacks by political leaders or publics of member states.[42] This direct relation between particular ministries or offices of member governments and specialized agencies hobbles co-ordination efforts because each specialized agency knows that it needs to keep its own particular clientele happy.

The Economic and Social Council was eclipsed from the start, and this became clearer as the Third World coalition began coalescing in the late 1950s. Though also established as a "principal organ," governments have always tended to treat ECOSOC as subordinate to the assembly and to reserve their best ideas for presentation in the latter. Particularly when it included only 18 member states but even after later expansions, states not represented on ECOSOC used the assembly to advance their views on social and economic questions, scrutinize ECOSOC's work, and frequently revise it significantly. This preference for using the assembly became a regular feature of Third World coalition politics. Even after expansion of ECOSOC from 18 to 27 members in 1963 and again to 54 in 1973 (a change that assured it a controling majority), the Third World majority bypassed it in favor of new, whole membership bodies like UNCTAD, and the UN Industrial Development Organization. This bypassing suited the major Western industrial states, which were anxious to guard the autonomy of GATT, the IMF, and the World Bank.

This combination of disuse by governments and organizational self-protection by specialized agencies has prevented emergence of serious co-ordination efforts. In the 1977 debates on UN restructuring, the Third World majority ignored ECOSOC in its vision of a General Assembly-directed UN system provided with steady financial resources through an increased regular budget and reorganized to bring about and run the New International Economic Order. Western industrial states were concerned primarily with making each separate program more efficient, and were not prepared to turn UN bodies or elements of the UN Secretariat into agencies of the NIEO or to subordinate the specialized agencies and economic institutions to the General Assembly. The Soviet bloc was pulled in two directions: it also wanted to avoid increases in the UN budget, but was not averse to reorganizations that would reduce Western influence in the UN system.

Only as South–North confrontation abated in the late 1980s, did conditions become conducive to serious discussion of improving co-ordination. Yet discussions so far have not resulted in dramatic measures. The most elaborate and coherent reform proposal came in 1991 from the Nordic states, countries that could not be accused of "UN bashing" or lacking sympathy for Third

World aspirations.[43] Their proposal included several major changes: 1) increasing the amount of official development assistance channeled through the voluntary UN programs of UNDP, UNFPA, UNICEF, the World Food Program, and UNEP; 2) creating a single development assistance board to oversee all the development bodies; 3) creating a relatively small, approximately twenty-five-member, ministerial body to address all major international issues not handled in the Security Council; 4) substituting an Economic and Social Council made up of all UN member states for the assembly's Second and Third Committees; 5) restructuring the Specialized Agencies by replacing their plenary assemblies with smaller governing bodies composed of senior officials from each member's national development agency; and 6) financing development activities through a combination of assessments, periodic negotiated pledges on the model of World Bank replenishments, and voluntary contributions from governments. Though incorporating some long-standing proposals, the Nordic proposal suggested two sweeping changes. The first would have effectively merged ECOSOC into the General Assembly. The second would have reined in the specialized agencies, the Bretton Woods institutions, and GATT by eliminating their separate plenary bodies and subordinating them to the reorganized assembly.

While very attractive to advocates of UN reform, and inspiring considerable positive comments in the academic literature, very little of the Nordic proposal was adopted, and the development-centered elements disappeared with almost no trace.[44] Discussion of reform continues, but results – whether of the greater efficiency sought by the West or the more coherent structure sought by others – remain slight. Even the new Chief Executives Board for Co-ordination composed of senior staff acting for the heads of the specialized agencies, the Bretton Woods institutions, and the WTO has made little difference.[45] The strength of the policy networks surrounding the Specialized Agencies, and Third World governments' greater readiness to engage in the Bretton Woods institutions and the WTO directly, have reinforced institutional decentralization. The High Level Panel on Treats, Challenges, and Change has recognized this in proposing that ECOSOC focus on providing normative and analytical leadership on economic development issues and prodding states to assess their progress toward development goals in "an open and transparent manner."[46]

The General Assembly and the UN Secretariat

The UN Charter includes the Secretariat among the "principal organs" and gives the Secretary-General the right to call the Security Council's attention to any situation likely to threaten international peace and security. The Charter also includes some broad stipulations about the Secretariat, but leaves the details of size, internal organization, and composition to be determined by the General Assembly. Thus a Secretary-General must be able to work with and maintain the confidence of the assembly as well as of the council.

The General Assembly and the Secretary-General

The Charter specifies that the Security Council recommends appointment of a particular person as Secretary-General, with the appointment effective if the General Assembly then accepts that recommendation. Because the veto applies to Security Council recommendations, the assembly majority knows that any candidate it desires must pass muster with all five permanent members. Conversely, the Permanent 5 know that they must name a candidate acceptable to a majority in the assembly. Thus each of the Permanent 5 and the assembly majority has equal leverage in the highly political process of selecting a Secretary-General. The sharp politics involved in appointing or discarding a Secretary General have been obvious almost from the start. The first Secretary-General, Trygvie Lie, lost the confidence of the Soviet Union in 1953 and was forced into resignation. The second, Dag Hammarskjöld, was generally acceptable because he came from a neutral country (Sweden) and his record as a civil servant suggested that he would be a competent administrator but not take any particular political initiative. Hammarskjöld soon disconfirmed that prediction. His early initiatives in developing peacekeeping won general support, but his conduct of the Congo operation met with strong opposition from the Soviet Union and was questioned by other important member states. The Soviets first expressed their dissatisfaction by proposing a "troika" – substituting a committee of three (one from the Soviet bloc, one from the Western bloc, and one from the neutral and Nonaligned) for the single Secretary-General. The Afro-Asian, Latin American, and Western groups all rejected this idea. However, when it came time to find a successor to Hammarskjöld, they did agree on the selection of a less activist candidate, U Thant of Burma. While the political pushes and pulls surrounding appointment of the Secretary-General have been public knowledge each time, the struggle was most spectacular in 1996. That year, after failing to persuade Boutros Boutros-Ghali to fulfill his earlier promise to step down after one term, the US government imposed a highly publicized veto on his reappointment. The rest of the UN membership was unhappy,[47] but realized it had no choice in the matter. The African group did salvage something from the collision in winning agreement that, because Boutros-Ghali had only served one term, his successor should also come from Africa. In 2004 some US conservatives and others demanded Kofi Annan's resignation after public revelations of kickbacks and other abuses in the UN's "oil-for-food" program allowing certain sales of Iraqi oil, which was supervised by the Secretariat's Department of Peacekeeping Operations while he headed it. Others, including the George W. Bush administration, supported his continuation in office.

The General Assembly and the rest of the Secretariat

Article 100 of the Charter specifies that other members of the Secretariat are appointed by the Secretary-General under regulations established by the General Assembly. The rest are divided into two groups, the "political appointees" at the Deputy, Under, and Assistant Secretary-General ranks, and the career professional and general service posts (D1–2 and P1–5 in the UN organizational charts). Following League of Nations precedent, the UN Charter established a truly international Secretariat, consisting of individual appointees serving for long periods and formally obliged by Article 100 to neither seek nor accept instructions "from any government or from any other authority external to the Organization." These provisions suggest that the organization should recruit staff directly, but member governments have often had other ideas. Some, particularly among the Soviet bloc, insisted that the UN select staff from a list of candidates they prepared. Others, including the US government, allowed the organization to recruit but insisted on subjecting potential appointees to background checks before they were employed.

Article 101 specifies that "the paramount consideration in the employment of the staff and in the determination of the conditions of service shall be the necessity of securing the highest standards of efficiency, competence, and integrity. Due regard shall be paid to the importance of recruiting staff on as wide a geographical basis as possible." Member governments have emphasized geographical spread more heavily than Article 101 suggests. The rush to put the organization together in 1945–6 had created a Secretariat of which two-thirds were US, British, or French nationals. Both the Soviet bloc and the Latin American group were anxious to get their nationals into places on the Secretariat, and strongly supported developing some sort of formula that would insure a sharing-out of appointments at all ranks. In the 1940s and 1950s, most attention was paid to the top level positions, and informal agreements that particular senior positions should be filled by a national of a particular country soon took hold.

The Third World majority took a different approach, extending to all the career ranks the same emphasis on "equitable geographical distribution" that marked its approach to apportioning seats on General Assembly committees and other bodies. While African governments paid little attention to getting their nationals into the Secretariat during the 1960s,[48] they heeded Algerian Foreign Minister Abdelaziz Bouteflika's 1974 remark that "the only thing left now to decolonize is the Secretariat."[49] Though giving each member state a specific quota of Secretariat appointments had been rejected in 1945, the Third World majority was able to build on the looser system of "desirable ranges" that initially allocated appointments by the size of a state's contribution to the budget. In 1962, under Third World pressure, U Thant proposed, and the General Assembly accepted, a formula reserving five appointments for nationals of each member state, and then took population as well as budget contribution into account. Continuing Third World pressures led to weighing population more heavily in later iterations of the formula. The present formula uses the fact of membership to distribute 40 percent (1,080) of the 2,700 posts covered by the system, share of regular budget assessments to distribute 55 percent (1,485) of them, and a bonus for high population to distribute the remaining 5 percent (135).[50]

These arguments about staff recruitment focus primarily on the higher ranks; all, including the Third World majority, accept that clerical and maintenance employees will be drawn primarily from the city where a particular UN headquarters is located. For appointments to posts at the highest ranks – the Under and Assistant Secretaries-General, and directors of Secretariat units – the desirable range system is supplemented by informal "national reservations" that hold certain posts for nationals of a particular state. These began to develop in 1945 with an understanding that each permanent member of the Security Council would have one national among the Under Secretaries, and the practice later spread to additional posts. Though securing assembly resolutions condemning the notion that particular career posts "belong" to any state or group of states, the Third World majority did endorse the idea that replacements for persons appointed on short-term contracts should come from the same country or region when needed to maintain the desirable ranges.[51] Thus the pressure to gain hold over particular posts continues to coexist with Third World pressure for drawing those persons staffing the higher levels of the Secretariat from a wider array of countries.

These pressures to distribute posts among a wider group of nationalities, together with the UN's long budget crisis after 1985, promoted greater reliance on short-term appointments. Hammarskjöld had used short-term appointments to diversify the Secretariat, and his successor U Thant extended the practice to the point that more than 34 percent of the professional staff held short-term appointments in 1969.[52] The proportion of professional staff on short-term appointments continued to rise in the 1970s. When the UN became more active in conflict resolution and humanitarian assistance in the 1990s, several observers endorsed heavy use of short-term appointments to recruit into the Secretariat persons with the sorts of skills needed for those activities. At the same time, the inertia in favor of a career service remains strong, not least among the staff itself because the UN pension system strongly favors lengthy service.

The Charter says nothing about the size, internal organization, or composition of the Secretariat other than that "appropriate staffs shall be permanently assigned to the Economic and Social Council, the Trusteeship Council, and, as required, to other organs of the United Nations." The initial Secretariat organizational chart was heavily influenced by League of Nations practice. In subsequent years, the General Assembly usually accepted the Secretary-General's proposals on organizational rearrangements, and left staff recruitment to him and his subordinates. Individual governments have influenced recruiting of their own nationals, and a significant part of the early spirit of the UN Secretariat was destroyed as Secretary-General Lie co-operated closely with McCarthyite loyalty investigations of US nationals in the Secretariat.[53] Other governments were more subtle, screening applicants before they could apply for positions and keeping many of them on short-term contracts.[54]

Sprawling bureaucracy and unco-ordinated effort have been the subject laments since the 1950s. They never became major issues for the US-led majority because the Secretariat and the budget were relatively small. Aside from the highly intrusive US loyalty investigations, the US-led majority was most concerned with creating and staffing certain new UN bodies, such as the International Atomic Energy Agency and the Commission on Human Rights. The Third World majority took reorganization a step further in the late 1960s when it began mandating the establishment of special Secretariat units to handle particular questions, such as the UNCTAD Secretariat, the UNIDO Staff, or the Unit on Palestinian Rights.

The phrase "bureaucratic sprawl" became a byword for the UN among outsiders in the 1970s and early 1980s as special units proliferated and studies seeking to identify more effective organizational structures and practices were undertaken inside and outside the UN. Critics of the UN looked at increasing staff numbers, or externally developed indicators of how much of the staff did effective work, to argue that the Secretariat was overstaffed, over-rewarded, and underworked.[55] Faced with the first round of US withholdings, Perez de Cuellar implemented suggestions from a UN-commissioned study in 1986[56] and realized considerable savings. Other adjustments were made in the 1990s as budgets continued to be tight and demands for UN involvement in peacekeeping and conflict resolution rose. Secretary-General Annan was able to elicit assembly support for a significant reorganization. On his own initiative and in reaction to the severe budget crunch imposed by US and other members' laggard payments, he began grouping the Secretariat into larger theme-based units, ultimately establishing five main clusters of peace and security, UN development group, humanitarian affairs, economic and social, and general services.[57] In 2002 he also won assent for the long-discussed step of appointing a Deputy Secretary-General to help manage the organization. In 2003, the UN's permanent employees were 25 percent fewer than they had been in 1997,[58] but in some areas better qualified because growing talent pools allowed Annan to give greater weight to relevant expertise and experience.

Debate about how large a Secretariat the UN needs has been constant since the early 1970s. Critics point to real and alleged inefficiencies and corruption to suggest that the Secretariat is too large and packed with underqualified individuals put in place because of connections. Defenders maintain that the Secretariat compares favorably with most national bureaucracies and suggest by comparisons to the number of persons serving in the New York City police, one of the smaller US states, or some European city's administration that the Secretariat is tiny indeed. Given the different administrative tasks involved, these comparisons are beside the point. More relevant are assessments determining how many people are needed to run effective peacekeeping and humanitarian assistance operations, provide effective economic and technical aid, and help governments build administrative capacity.

The General Assembly in world politics

The General Assembly seems most influential when its resolutions recommend what member states already want to do. However, its real influence depends on whether the normative principles and causal beliefs advocated in its resolutions become and remain credible to enough member states that they become the general international practice. The assembly appears to have more control over other elements of the UN system. Yet even within the organization it shares authority with the Security Council on some matters (admission and expulsion of member states; appointment of the Secretary-General), has not been able to overcome the independence of the Specialized Agencies, GATT and its successor WTO, or the Bretton Woods Institutions, and often depends heavily on the Secretariat for information and ideas.

The General Assembly has far less authority and influence in the international system than a legislature has in its national political system. Those who believe that the best way to attain global peace is to replicate at the global level the centralized political institutions found within nations thus regard the assembly as falling far short of what is desirable. Yet even observers less in thrall to the "domestic analogy" and more attuned to the possibilities of improving decentralized co-operation complain about the assembly. These criticisms are taken up in Chapter 5.

Notes

1   Any doubt about this ended with seating of Beijing's delegates as representatives of China in 1971 and admission of East and West Germany to membership in 1973.

2 For example, statements by US, Soviet, and Canadian delegations indicating that their governments accepted as binding the rules in General Assembly Resolution 1962 (XVIII) of 13 December 1963, the Declaration of Legal Principles governing the Activities of States in the Exploration and Use of Outer Space in A/C.1/SR.1342 (2 December 1963), 159 and 161; A/C.1/SR.1346 (5 December 1963), 161; and A/18/PV.1280.

3 The 1947 Peace Treaty between the Allies and Italy stipulated that if the parties could not agree on the disposition of Italy's colonies, they would submit the question to the General Assembly for decision. After negotiations failed, they took the question to the assembly, which settled the matter in Resolution 289 (IV) of 21 November 1949.

4 The Charter also gave the General Assembly authority to approve Trusteeship Agreements (except those relating to "strategic areas," which are approved by the Security Council), but no additional Trust Territories have been designated since 1950.

5 Advisory Opinion on the Competence of the General Assembly Regarding Admission to the United Nations, 3 March 1950, *ICJ Reports of Judgments, Advisory Opinions and Orders 1950*, 7.

6 E.g. GA Resolutions 197 (III) of 8 December 1948 and 296 (IV) of 22 November 1949, commenting on the East–West stalemate on new members.

7 GA Resolution 1514 (XV) of 14 December 1960.

8 "The representation of China at the UN," *Harvard International Law Journal* 12(3): 478–94 (1971).

9 Linda Fasulo, *An Insider's Guide to the UN* (New Haven, CT: 2004), 99, notes that a minority of member states have expressed support for a "two Chinas" position. Beijing did accept a "two Chinas" solution in WTO on condition the ROC use the name "Chinese Taipei."

10 Suellen Ratliffe, "UN representation disputes," *California Law Review* 87(5): 1207–64 (1999), also covers the 1973–5 and 1997 controversies.

11 United Nations *Repertory of Practice of United Nations Organs*, Supplement 3, vol. 1, 211.

12 A/28/PV.2141 (5 October 1973), par. 44.

13 A/29/PV.2281 (30 September 1974), par. 12–86.

14 M.J. Peterson, *The General Assembly in World Politics* (London: 1986), 123.

15 GA Resolution 47/1 of 22 September 1992.

16 This was clearest in the late 1940s when US GDP was more than 40 percent of world product, but remains true in 2005.

17 Adopted to carry UNEF II through 1974 in GA Resolution 3101 (XXVIII) of 11 December 1973.

18 Gert Rosenthal, "The scale of assessments of the UN budget," *Global Governance* 10(3): 357 (July–September 2004).

19 Klaus Hufner, "Financing the United Nations," in Dennis Dijkzeul and Yves Beigbeider (eds), *Rethinking International Organizations* (Oxford and New York: 2003), 29.

20 Parliamentary Debates, House of Commons, fifth series, vol. 651, col. 755; also quoted in Inis L. Claude, Jnr, "The political framework of the UN's financial problems," *International Organization* 17: 850 (1963).

21 Hernane Tavares de Sa, *The Play within the Play: The Inside Story of the United Nations* (New York: 1966), 49.

22 UN Doc. A/5916/Add. 1 (16 August 1965) in *General Assembly Official Records, 19th Session, Annexes*, vol. 2, Agenda Item 21, 86.

23 Hufner, "Financing the United Nations," 41.
24 Explanations of vote in A/41/PV.102 (19 December 1986).
25 See Rosenthal, "The scale of assessments of the UN budget," for the details.
26 Hufner, "Financing the United Nations," 38 and 46–8.
27 Scale of assessments adopted in GA Resolution 55/5B-F of 23 December 2000.
28 Paul Taylor, "Developing the role of ECOSOC," in Paul Taylor and A.J.R. Groom (eds), *The United Nations at the Millennium: The Principal Organs* (London: 2000), 138.
29 GA Resolution 217 (III) of 10 December1948.
30 GA Resolution 2131(XX) of 21 December 1965.
31 Charles Maynes, "The United Nations in today's world," in Tobi Trister Gati (ed.), *The US, the UN, and the Management of Global Change* (1983), 334–5.
32 GA Resolution 3379 (XXX) of 10 November 1975.
33 By GA Resolution 46/86 of 16 December 1991.
34 The phrases used by Kishore Mahbubani, "The United Nations and the United States," in David Malone and Yuen Foong Khong (eds) *Unilateralism and US Foreign Policy: International Perspectives* (Boulder: 2003), 141.
35 By Resolution 377 (V) of 11 November 1950.
36 See Richard L. Jackson, *The Nonaligned, the UN, and the Superpowers* (New York: 1983), Chapter 3.
37 For example the operative part of General Assembly Resolution 47/120B of 20 September 1974 (the last day of a resumed session); Humphrey Assisi-Asobie, "Nigeria and the United Nations," in Chadwick Alger, Gene M. Lyons, and John E. Trent (eds), *The United Nations System: The Policies of Member States* (Tokyo: 1995), 341; Erskine Childers quoted in Michael G. Schechter, "The United Nations in the aftermath of Somalia," in Edwin M. Smith and Michael G. Schechter (eds), *The United Nations in a New World Order* (Claremont, CA: 1994), 79, note 20.
38 Blanche Finley, *The Structure of the General Assembly* (Dobbs Ferry, NY: 1977), vol. i, 182 and 202.
39 See Michael G. Schechter, *UN Global Conferences* (London: 2005).
40 The version animating the Charter's drafters was laid out in David Mitrany, *A Working Peace System* (London: 1943).
41 Leon Gordenker, "Development of the UN System," in Tobi Tister Gati (ed.), *The US, the UN and the Management of Global Change* (New York: 1983), 23.
42 See, e.g., Robert W. Cox, "The executive head," *International Organization* 23(2): 205–30 (1969); Robert W. Cox and Harald S. Jacobson (eds), *The Anatomy of Influence* (New Haven: 1973).
43 The Nordic UN Project, *The United Nations in Development, Final Report* (Stockholm: 1991).
44 Noted acidly by Marie-Claude Smouts, "UN reform: a strategy of avoidance," in Michael G. Schechter (ed.), *Innovation in Multilateralism* (Tokyo: 1999), 33–4.
45 Created in 2000 to replace the older Administrative Co-ordination Council. See *www.un.org/*.
46 High Level Panel on Threats, Challenges, and Change, *A More Secure World: Our Shared Responsibility*, par. 274–81.
47 Expressed most immediately by declining to elect a US national to the Advisory Committee on Administrative and Budgetary Questions for the first time in UN history.
48 Tavares de Sa, *The Play within the Play* (New York: 1966), 124.

49 Quoted in L. Jackson, *The Nonaligned, the UN, and the Superpowers*, 159.
50 Anthony Mango, "Personnel and administration," *Issues before the General Assembly*, 2003–4, p.274.
51 GA Resolution 35/210 of 17 December 1980, par. 4.
52 See UN Doc. A/7745 (5 November 1969), 11.
53 See, e.g., Yves Beigbeder, *Threats to the International Service* (London: 1988), 47–56.
54 Soviet bloc states were particularly adept at these practices. See Beigbeder, *Threats to the International Civil Service*, 66–81.
55 For example, Houshang Ameri, *Fraud, Waste and Abuse* (Washington, DC: 2003).
56 Report of the Group of High-Level Intergovernmental Experts to Review the Efficiency of the Administrative and Financial Functioning of the UN, UN Doc. A/41/49 (15 August 1986). See assembly endorsement of most of its suggestions in GA Resolution 41/213 of 19 December 1986.
57 See the organizational chart on the UN website at *www.un.org/reform/track2/ initiate.htm#newun*.
58 *Yearbook of the United Nations, 1999*, p. 1330 and *2001*, p. 1342.

5 Key criticisms of the General Assembly in historical perspective

The only political institutions attracting no criticism are those that everyone dismisses as irrelevant. The fact that national political leaders, policy experts, intellectuals, and ordinary citizens find fault with the UN General Assembly says that it still matters to them. It is the extent and substance of criticism that indicates whether a political institution is in serious trouble and likely to be replaced, or still enjoys enough respect that it can carry out its functions while members of the political community argue about whether or how to reform it.

Proposals for "reforming," "improving," and "revitalizing," the General Assembly – and the UN system as a whole – have been made for decades, and grew in number after the end of the Cold War. Improving the management of security issues and the global economy have absorbed most of the reforming energy, and many discussions of how the UN could be improved in those areas pay little or no attention to the General Assembly.[1] In the current discussions, most of which at least give passing attention to the General Assembly, the criticisms echo themes that have been sounded in varying degrees since 1945.

Today the General Assembly attracts four main criticisms. The first complains that it is captive to the mechanical politics of an "automatic majority" able to summon up a two-thirds vote for any proposition, regardless of its intellectual, moral, or political merit, and grinding out nearly identical resolutions year after year regardless of whether those resolutions say anything helpful on the issue addressed. The second dismisses it as an "ineffectual talk shop" where delegates treat each other to dull speeches and spend lots of time in and outside the meeting hall haggling intensely over minor changes in the wording of resolutions that are meaningless to anyone outside, won't be read, and won't be acted upon. The third makes an opposite complaint, that the General Assembly is all too effective in spreading values contrary to those on which the Charter is based and inimical to creating a better world. The fourth insists that the General Assembly's legitimacy is seriously eroded by the "democratic deficit" resulting from the lack of a clear line of connection or accountability between the peoples of the member states and the delegates in the assembly. Each of these criticisms comes in several versions, some more reasonably stated than others, and enjoys enough currency to merit examination before considering in Chapter 6 how the assembly might be reconfigured to operate more effectively.

One criticism commonly raised against some UN bodies is never raised against the assembly: no one complains that it has been "politicized." Such complaint is reasonable when raised against a body that is supposed to make decisions based on some other logic – for instance the legal reasoning used by a court or the expert reasoning used by a technical commission. However, the General Assembly is a political body, and participants have never pretended otherwise. Rather, they accept and take advantage of that character. As one senior delegate is said to have told subordinates getting ready for a session in the 1950s, "whenever possible, use good political arguments. If there are no good political arguments, use bad political arguments. If there are no bad political arguments, use legal arguments."[2] There is much complaint about the content and quality of the assembly's resolutions, but even those who do not like the results accept that the assembly is a political deliberative body.

Captured by an automatic majority

One of the oldest complaints about the General Assembly says that it is the home of an "automatic majority," – a stable and long-lasting coalition of member states able to muster a two-thirds majority whenever it wishes. Such complaints, which invariably come from governments outside, or persons not fully sympathetic with, the prevailing majority, reflect a belief that any coalition aware that it can muster the necessary votes at any time will largely ignore the opinions and interests of other states.

The empirical evidence for the existence of an automatic majority during most of the assembly's existence is very strong. Mathematical roll-call analysis has simply confirmed with sophisticated social science methodology what every delegate in the assembly has known. Until the mid-1950s the US government could round up a majority on almost any issue and even in the 1960s could set the terms of resolutions on Cold War-related political issues. Since the late 1960s a Third World majority has controlled the assembly whenever all its members worked together. Thus there is no doubt that automatic majorities have existed; the question is what that existence means for the member states and for the General Assembly itself.

The tendency to complain about an automatic majority dominating the assembly reflects the character of the international system, and highlights one way in which international politics still differs from national politics. In most national legislatures, whether the rubber-stamp body of a single-party state or the freely elected assembly of a multiparty state, there is an automatic majority. A single-party regime goes to great lengths to assure itself an automatic majority by preventing people from voting for anyone else. Parliamentary systems on the European model, in which the executive is selected from the leaders of the majority party of coalition in the legislature, assume the existence of an automatic majority. In such countries, legislative rejection of an important proposition favored by the executive amounts to a "loss of confidence" requiring the executive to resign. The executive's position can be precarious if two or more parties have to form a coalition to become a legislative majority, but as long as the coalition holds it is assured an automatic majority. Only in countries, including many Latin American republics and the USA, where the executive and legislative branches are elected separately is there no built-in automatic majority backing the executive. The executive has to eke out support issue by issue and may well see its policy preferences ignored or overridden by an unsympathetic legislative majority.

Where they exist, national automatic majorities are accepted as a fact of political life. The single-party form of automatic majority may be resented, but citizens realize that expressing that resentment can be dangerous so keep quiet or use elliptical expressions designed to elude censors and police. In a stable democracy, the sense of common national identity provides a check on majorities and minorities alike, encouraging each to regard the other as a responsible rival rather than an implacable enemy. Democracies also institutionalize safeguards for individual and minority rights, and turn politics into an ongoing interaction by holding periodic free elections that offer today's minorities the possibility of becoming the whole or a part of the majority in the future. Safeguards and iteration reduce the stakes of each individual vote or election by establishing limits on government action and an ongoing process in which majorities and minorities are likely to change places over time.

Automatic majorities inspire more discomfort at the international level because the sense of common human identity remains weak. National delegates in the General Assembly regard themselves as agents of their state charged with advancing its interests. Most develop a greater sense of the mutuality, reciprocity, or parallel nature of different states' interests than shared by their superiors at home, but even they do not as yet share a sufficiently strong sense of global (or cosmopolitan) identity to subordinate national interest to it. Thus there is no global equivalent to the shared national identity serving as a check on pursuit of more local constituencies' interests that Edmund Burke identified in 1774 as the essential foundation of a well-functioning national legislature.[3] Nor is there confidence, despite safeguards in the assembly rules, that minority rights will be respected. Notions of sovereign equality of states and nonintervention provide some loose parallel to domestic-level individual and minority rights, but emphasize states' autonomy in ways that create tension with a sense of global identity. Thus any coalition of states able to form a stable assembly majority is not going to be trusted by the states outside, particularly when their opinions diverge significantly.

The experiences of isolated states suggest that consistently out-voted minorities in the assembly would have had an even harder time if they had not possessed sufficient capability outside the assembly to protect their interests and/or affect the extent to which assembly recommendations could be implemented. The US-led majority was fully aware that confrontation could not be pushed too far even before the Soviet Union acquired rough nuclear parity with USA in the late 1960s. Verbal barbs could be flung with abandon, but direct confrontation – particularly in Europe – had to be avoided lest it escalate into major war. Similarly, the Third World coalition is aware of – and greatly frustrated by – its lack of sufficient capability to carry out its own recommendations.

The amount of complaining about automatic majorities from national leaders and officials is clearly related to their country's current experiences in the assembly. The Soviet bloc was still minority in the 1970s and 1980s, but less uncomfortable with the Third World majority then by the US-led one. Explicit Soviet complaint about automatic majorities declined significantly, though did not quite go away because the Third World majority's views frequently diverged from Soviet ones. French complaints about automatic majorities[4] were greatest when France faced assembly condemnations over the Algerian War, and declined later when French governments perceived adopting a more friendly approach to the Third World as a way to offer the world an alternative to US leadership.[5] US complaints about automatic majorities emerged in the 1970s, as the decline in US influence in the assembly intersected with a rise of left-wing radicalism around the world.[6] Though many US observers have noted the Third World shift towards greater pragmatism since the late 1980s, US neoconservatives pick on certain continuing Third World stances or Third World disinclination to simply accept whatever the US government proposes to maintain their complaints about automatic majorities.

Ineffective talk shop

Complaints that the General Assembly is "an ineffectual talk shop" can be understood in two ways. The phrase could be understood as meaning that the assembly talks instead of taking action. This is grossly unfair because it was never designed to be an executive body. It was already far too large for that task in 1945, and was never provided with the command over resources and staff that would permit it to discharge executive tasks. National political leaders around the world know very well that the power to tax is the power to shape the community, and have carefully kept that power in their own hands. Thus the member governments have carefully avoided giving the assembly (or any other part of the UN system) the authority to levy taxes on their citizens or corporations, and kept the UN dependent on member states' contributions. They also established an additional safeguard by including budget and assessments decisions among the "important questions" requiring a two-thirds majority. In 1986, the required supermajority was increased when they further agreed that budget and assessments would be determined by consensus.

Keeping the budget modest by national standards also ensures that the United Nations does not develop a large administrative apparatus capable of reaching directly to their populations. Even the Third World governments most interested in increasing the level of UN resources and staff devoted to development activities have been very nervous about recent trends toward increased co-operation between UN staffers and NGOs, and not always particularly enthusiastic about NGO participation in global conferences and their follow-up sessions.

Thus it is unfair to complain that inability to do anything but talk makes the General Assembly useless. Political systems need deliberative institutions no less than executive and administrative ones, particularly in a historical era when norms of transparent decision-making following open debate are widely supported. The relevant meaning of "talk shop," and the potential ground for justifiable criticism, focuses on the effective performance of deliberative functions.

Yet it is entirely legitimate to ask whether the General Assembly fulfills its deliberative functions well under its current procedures, or could do better under other procedures. While pursuing this inquiry, it is important to remember that procedures that appear workable in abstract logic are not always as successful when applied in a real human community riven by ideological disagreements, cultural differences, historical resentments, and emotional currents that often make it difficult for deliberators to proceed in the basically rational way most philosophers of deliberative democracy posit as the ideal. All of the traditions of group deliberation around the world, including the Western traditions of parliamentary procedure from which many of the assembly's rules derive, are efforts to foster modes of discussion effectively balancing each participant's right to be heard with the group's need to resolve (however temporarily) the issue at hand.

Understanding the phrase "ineffectual talk shop" to mean "poorly functioning deliberative body" shifts attention to how well the General Assembly serves as a deliberative body. On this criterion, it deserves considerable criticism even after allowing for the challenges posed by an increasing membership

and a lengthening agenda, and the strains on ability to function as a deliberative organ that each imposes. More member states means a larger number of
delegations needing opportunities to express their views at meetings and
participate in informal consultations. More member states also increases the
number of like-minded needed to form a simple majority, a two-thirds
majority, or a consensus. The assembly has responded to this challenge by
developing the system of regional groups and other caucuses permitting
broadly like-minded delegations to operate as a group and negotiate with other
cohesive groupings rather than having to approach every individual delegation
on every question. Wise delegations do know that certain delegations must be
approached individually on almost every question, and that on any particular
question there are a few others with special interests or expertise who should
also be consulted individually. However, the caucuses make the problem of
negotiating in a body of 191 delegations far more tractable than it would be
otherwise. Growing reliance on informal consultations, particularly for
working out the details of proposals, means there is more time in formal meetings for hearing everyone's views. The ability to shift between the formal rules
of majority voting and the informal rules of operating by consensus allows the
assembly to expedite matters when there is broad agreement, but also to
permit individual delegations or groups of delegations to take determined
stances when they desire. With the Cold War over, and the economic differences among Third World states widening, the regional caucuses do not have
as much political logic as they had in the 1960s and 1970s. However, the need
to have some form of groupings among delegations means caucuses will reform rather than disappear.

While incremental adjustments of procedures and expansions of the group
caucusing system have been reasonably effective in coping with increases in
membership, incremental change has been less effective in coping with the
ever-lengthening agenda. Looking only at the numbered items on the agenda,
the General Assembly has gone from handling 108 items at its first session in
1946 to handling 165 at its 58th in 2003.[7] The press of more items has
prompted several incremental adjustments of working methods. The shift to
working out proposals during informal consultations reduced the number and
length of formal meetings, and allowed a more freely flowing discussion.
General limits on the number or length of various types of speeches in formal
meetings have also helped move deliberation along, though sometimes at the
expense of forcing very cramped statements of views. The assembly has also
carved out additional work time by resuming sessions in the spring, though
this quickly runs up against the time demands of other UN bodies.
Transferring the writing of major multilateral treaties and periodic deliberation on particular global issues to special UN conferences has spread the
work, but also contributed to the assembly's eclipse by drawing attention

elsewhere. The increasing number of assembly subsidiary bodies spreads work and creates additional meeting time, but also contributes to impressions of sprawl and incoherence.

Yet the assembly has been unwilling to look squarely at its situation and develop methods of focusing its work more effectively. The Fourth Committee, one of the most active during the earlier phases of decolonization, was left with almost nothing to do for more than 20 years before being merged with the Special Political Committee. A long line of proposals to redefine the relation among the General Assembly plenary, the Second and Third Committees, and the Economic and Social Council have gone nowhere despite wide agreement that the UN system's methods of handling economic issues and development assistance are too diffuse to be effective. In fairness to the assembly, it should be noted that the self-protective instincts of the specialized agencies and other UN entities, and the preferences of both developing and industrial states for handling economic issues in other forums (not always the same ones), have also frustrated significant change.

The assembly has adopted some minor forms of agenda control. The Fifth Committee's 1970 adoption of "biennialization" for budget and staff issues was emulated in the Second and Third Committees during the 1990s. The First and Fourth Committees have been more reluctant to alternate agenda items. The First deals with disarmament, and many delegations seem to feel that constant pressure must be maintained if the end of the Cold War is to translate into any significant reduction in armaments. The Fourth now deals with the hot political issues not taken up in plenary, and delegates are reluctant to omit any of them lest omission be taken as a sign of decreased interest or as a change in majority opinion about the merits of the issue.

The assembly has tried some experiments in highlighting certain issues by holding "high-level dialogues" or "thematic discussions." It has also organized more and more decennial or quinquennial reviews of major programs, like the UN Development Decades, the Programme of Action adopted at the World Social Summit in 1997, or the Millennium Development Goals. However, these additions to its agenda have not disturbed the basic tendency to leave issues on the agenda year after year. Occasionally, this reluctance to drop items appears merited in hindsight: the delegations most eager to keep the Palestinian question on the agenda, even while the peace process appeared to be engaged in the mid-1990s, felt justified by its collapse after 1998. In other cases, as with the annual debate on "the activities of foreign economic and other interests" inhibiting decolonization, assembly consideration appears unrelated to events.

Even with greater willingness to distinguish between "resolutions" making statements on the substantive issues of the day and "decisions" settling internal assembly or UN questions, the expectation is that the assembly will adopt a resolution on the vast majority of agenda items before it invites dismissing them all as meaningless clutter. Delegates and others who closely follow the particular issue being addressed notice the changes, often subtle, in each year's formulation, but most people outside UN Headquarters find most of the differences too small to comprehend. Since there is already more than enough to read in the world, on-line or off, the assembly would be better served by speaking only when it has something notable to say.

Multiple resolutions on the same issue can create another problem: contradictory statements on the same question at the same time. This might reflect unease among the members, as with simultaneous adoption of resolutions endorsing the notion of free, competitive elections and resolutions re-emphasizing the importance of avoiding outside interference in member states' affairs adopted in 1989 and 1990.[8] It might reflect different dynamics in two main committees discussing overlapping issues because the plenary seldom changes the drafts emanating from the main committees. Two committees might have different drafts because the same point is contentious enough in one to be dropped to secure a consensus while less contentious in the other and remains in the draft. Differences might also stem from the fact different subcoalitions control the drafting in different committees or from the process by which a "committed" subsidiary organ steers drafting in the main committee to which it reports. Contradictions between Security Council and General Assembly resolutions can be confusing, but are easily explainable by the very different political dynamics of the two bodies; it takes a close observer to explain why the assembly seems to speak in many ways at once.

Some delegates do appear to be aware of the morass into which the assembly has settled, but have not found it easy to break the inertia impelling the assembly towards a new resolution on every matter each year. Instead, they have accepted the perception that an issue will draw greater public attention if it becomes the subject of a global conference or summit. This only pushes the assembly further into the background and confirms the inertia encouraging it to attempt covering an impossibly long agenda each year.

The General Assembly can regain prominence as a global deliberative body only by breaking with its accumulated inertia and admitting that it cannot hope to address adequately anywhere near the number of issues on its current agenda. Even those hoping the assembly will become a true global legislature should support this change. National legislatures do adopt a considerable body of law each year, but they never attempt to address every question that could be raised by anyone in the country. They also distinguish quite explicitly between the major issues requiring extended attention and the less salient matters requiring shorter bursts of legislative attention.

Any program of limiting the agenda must address the fact that the assembly as prime supervisor and organizer of the UN system needs to address a considerable number of organizational and supervisory matters each year to keep the UN machinery running. Using the distinction between "resolutions" and "decisions" to mark the routine actions off from more important deliberations more systematically would help media and publics understand its proceedings better.

The Economic and Social Council reorganized its sessions and began reducing the length of its agenda in 1992, when it explicitly divided its annual sessions into "organizational" and "substantive' phases, with the latter divided into consideration of operational matters and discussions of a selected thematic concern. Secretary-General Annan has been urging the General Assembly to adopt a similar procedure, but it has not yet gone beyond an occasional "forum" or "roundtable" segment.

Additionally, there are times when the chief global deliberative forum should not take a particular conflict off its agenda lest the actors involved conclude they now have a free hand to do as they please. However, the assembly could also use "decisions" to mark continued monitoring of an unchanged situation, and reserve "resolutions" for statements reacting to significant new developments or reflecting new ideas about how the conflict could be resolved.

Amplifier of noxious ideas

Some observers have concluded that the General Assembly is all too effective as a deliberative body – one promoting noxious ideas that if acted upon would worsen rather than improve the world. In recent years, such conclusions have been voiced most vociferously by US neoconservatives, but have always been staples of right-wing thought in the USA and elsewhere. This led some to refer to the UN as a "dangerous place."[9] In strong contrast to the Johnson and Nixon administrations, which seemed prepared to accept the General Assembly as it was and largely ignore its resolutions, neoconservatives saw the General Assembly as an important front in continuing Cold War competition where the USSR was winning many gains by default. As in their general critique of pursuing "*détente*" with the USSR, the neoconservatives chastised others for underestimating the impact of words and failing to object to pernicious resolutions. Though neoconservatives are often identified with the Reagan era reintensification of the Cold War, their influence remained strong after 1990 and revived considerably in the George W. Bush administration (2001–).

The basic neoconservative argument derives from accepting that the General Assembly is not only a political body, but also a place for verbal combat that cannot be ignored. Neoconservatives do not take solace from the comforting maxim that "sticks and stones may break my bones but words can never hurt me." Reacting to the highly ideological character of national and world politics in most of the twentieth century, they strongly believe in the centrality of ideas as political motivators.

Despite the considerable spread of democratic rule since the early 1980s, neoconservatives are still inclined to regard the assembly as populated mainly by delegates serving unrepresentative regimes anxious to maintain their domination at home by emphasizing the rights of states at the expense of the rights of individuals, and using criticisms of human rights as "Western-imposed values" to oppress their own people. Part of the neo-conservative distrust of the assembly can be traced to the Third World majority's adoption of a severely anti-Israeli stance in 1973–5. However, that was only one source of a more general irritation. The terms of the resolutions on the New International Economic Order actually adopted by the assembly were mild in comparison with the stridently anti-market and pro-statist rhetoric of the most vocal members of the Group of 77. Assembly indigna-tion about human rights seemed to be confined to the misdeeds of right-wing governments, except when special circumstances (such as the elements of Sino-Soviet competition that permitted giving attention to Cambodia after 1978) arose. While a few neoconservatives revised their views after 1991,[10] most continue to regard the General Assembly as a source of toxic ideas, to be hectored or ignored while the world's "sole remaining superpower" reconstructs the world.[11]

In its almost sixty years of existence, the General Assembly has endorsed a wide range of ideas, stated either in the form of an abstract declaration or in the form of commentary on particular issues or conflicts. The substantive ideas it expresses reflect the tides of opinion among political elites around the world. Debates in the assembly do not change those elite opinions immedi-ately, or even contribute much to the more general trends that reduce or increase the attractiveness of political or economic ideas over time.

The end of the Cold War reduced the intensity of assembly debates by decreasing the range of disagreement. There is no single worldview, no "end of ideology," but the range of differences on some key questions – the relative priorities among groups of human rights; the relations among states, markets, and societies; the openness or closedness of national societies to external contacts and transactions – has been reduced significantly. The highly individ-ualist and extremely *laissez-faire* among US neoconservatives may not see much difference between today's assembly debates and those of the 1970s, but for everyone else there is much greater room for mutual comprehension and dialog rather than a shouting match. A few issues where old reflexes remain strong aside, the assembly is amplifying much less noxious notions today. The assembly's ineffectiveness as a deliberative body is now a more serious short-coming than its potential for amplifying noxious ideas.

Democratic deficit

Complaints that the General Assembly suffers from a "democratic deficit" refer not to the substance of its resolutions but to the lack of connection between it and the peoples of the member states. The notion that institutional legitimacy depends on direct connection to the peoples of member states is a relatively new criterion of international organization effectiveness, one attracting more interest in the wake of spreading democratization at the national level.

The newness of the idea is manifest in its lack of direct expression in the UN Charter. Its preamble does begin with the phrase: "We the Peoples of the United Nations," and suggests that it is the peoples who establish the goals, define the principles, and declare their resolve to "combine our efforts to accomplish these aims." Yet before the preamble ends, the focus shifts to the governments which "[agree] to the present Charter of the United Nations and do hereby establish an international organization to be known as the United Nations." This shift of focus assumes that the governments represent the will of the peoples, but nowhere does the Charter define the basis of that assumption. Later Charter provisions do proclaim the "right of self-determination" and emphasize "respect for human rights and fundamental freedoms" but governments of various ideologies could and did claim that their domestic practices conformed to these ideals.

In 1945, the definition of "representative" was broad enough to accommodate liberal republics, traditional monarchies, Leninist one-party states, and a variety of authoritarian governments. The only governments regarded as manifestly unrepresentative were Fascists (even though this required forgetting that Mussolini's Fascists did well in Italian elections, and that Hitler's Nazi Party won the January 1933 German election) or colonial administrations. Most of the former had been defeated in the Second World War and their remnants dealt with outside the UN, while Franco's Spain remained under a cloud of suspicion and was not invited to the San Francisco Conference. The latter would be encouraged into dissolution by the Trusteeship system and the Declaration on Non-Self-Governing Territories. Ideological conflict as well as the international principles emphasizing sovereignty, self-determination, and nonintervention in the domestic affairs of states discouraged any further notions that some modes of governance qualify as representative or democratic while others do not.

The lack of attention to mechanisms of accountability can be seen in the oldest form of complaint that the assembly is "undemocratic," which focused on the contrast between the definitions of "democratic" at the international and the national levels. The assembly's one state–one vote rule is profoundly undemocratic if the center of concern is individuals in a world community rather than states in an international system because the states of the world have such vastly different populations.

Yet each of these senses of "democratic" rests on a long tradition. As it spread after 1920, the notion of self-determination of peoples reinforced the late nineteenth- and early twentieth-century attack on the European division of the world into "civilized" and "uncivilized" states, in which only the former (as defined by the European powers) were treated as equal members of the international community. Abolishing that distinction and extending the principle of sovereign equality states to all states regardless of the race or level of economic activity of their inhabitants was reasonably viewed as the basis of a more democratic international system. No longer would a handful of states exercise mastery over the rest of the world. Yet within countries, democratic movements were insisting on the equal dignity of individuals. Though highly restricted franchises were common in 1900, universal adult suffrage had become the norm by mid-century. States claiming to be democratic but restricting the suffrage, whether formally through the electoral law or informally through biased administration or acquiescence in private intimidation of certain persons, found their claim to being "democratic" increasingly challenged after 1950.

There was a tension between the state-centered definition of democratic equality at the international level inspiring the General Assembly's one state–one vote rule, and the person-centered definition of democratic equality from the start. Even when the assembly gathered for its first session in 1946, the disparities in the populations of member states were great. The population of China (the most populous UN member) numbered some 512 million while the population of Luxembourg (the least populous) numbered about 290,000, yielding a 1,770:1 ratio between them. The disparities became larger, particularly after admission of a significant number of very tiny states in the 1970s. There was some brief discussion in UN circles about whether admitting "mini-states" to membership was a good idea; reasonable observers – not just stuffy Western conservatives – asked whether a state with a total population of only a few thousand was really, as Article 4 of the Charter specifies, "able and willing" to fulfill the obligations of membership. However, the logic of sovereign equality of states prevailed, and the tiny states were admitted. This greatly increased the population disparities. In 2002, the population of China (not including Taiwan) was estimated at 1,291 million and the population of Tuvalu at 10,600, yielding a 122,000:1 ratio.

The extent of change is equally apparent in the median population of UN member states, a more revealing measure than simply taking the mean (or average population) because the median divides a set of data into equal halves. The median population of the UN membership is the number at which 50 percent of the member states have a higher population and the other 50 percent have a lower population. In 1946, the median was 7.3 million or about 0.39 percent of world population. In 2002 the medium was 5.93 million but those 5.93 million were only 0.098 percent of world population because of global population growth.[12]

Though attractive to outside observers for philosophical reasons, weighting General Assembly votes by population alone would have limited impact on either the identity of the majority or the gap between votes inside the assembly and capability outside today. China and India together have some 38 percent of the world's population; adding Brazil plus Indonesia brings the joint share to 44.24 percent. The Group of 77 plus China would continue to control the General Assembly, though the relative influence wielded by its regional and subregional clusters would shift significantly. This was recognized as early as 1964 by Ali Mazrui, who wrote, "many is an African who might in 1962 have settled for eight UN votes answerable to Mr. Nehru on the Katanga issue for every vote answerable to Lord Home. A few might even settled for, as it were, two Sukarnos for every DeGaulle on almost every issue discussed in the United Nations since 1960" before concluding that the number of African states meant that the continent had more influence under the one state–one vote rule.[13]

Allocating votes by population would eliminate one fanciful scenario. Doing so would mean that the 127 least populous countries of the world, which together comprise about 8 percent of world population, would not be able to form a two-thirds majority in the assembly. In actual voting, those 127 countries have not stood out against all other countries; rather they have either joined in assembly-wide consensuses or voted with their respective regional groups. Even if they did, allocating votes by population alone would not eliminate the votes–capability gap that casts such a shadow over the assembly's deliberations.

Neither the current distribution of military power nor the current distribution of economic activity corresponds even remotely to the distribution of world population. Thus the same problem of how to draw powerful countries into agreement with General Assembly resolutions would remain if votes were allocated by population. This leads many advocates of weighted voting to propose multi-element formulas, most often including existence as a state, share of world population, and share of world economic activity.[14]

Weighted voting rules would still leave the task of representing the people to government-appointed delegates, and therefore not address the current concern about lack of legitimacy. The discussions of "democratic deficit" that began in the 1980s are based on an assumption that the UN will acquire legitimacy only if its bodies have a direct connection to the peoples of the world. While some observers seem to regard nongovernmental organizations as providing such connections, the most ardent critics of the UN's "democratic deficit" want to redress it by replacing or supplementing the General Assembly with a popularly elected body.

Nongovernmental organizations existed before 1945, and several – particularly the international federations of labor unions – were involved in the discussions about creating the United Nations and sent observers to the San Francisco Conference. NGOs, specifically labor union federations and employers' associations, already had direct representation in the International Labor Organization. The Soviets hoped to give their favored trade union federation status on the Economic and Social Council equivalent to that of UN member states, but this aroused sharp opposition from other trade union federations as well as other governments. In the end, nongovernmental organizations were linked to the United Nations through the system of "consultative status" established under Article 71 of the Charter. Under it, NGOs interact most intensively with the Economic and Social Council, and have a more distant relation with the General Assembly. The Fourth Committee, dealing with conditions in Trust Territories and other colonies, made most frequent contact with individuals and NGOs through periodic meetings at which inhabitants of non-self-governing territories were invited to discuss conditions there.

Contacts between NGOs and other UN bodies began to increase in the 1970s with the first round of global conferences. Starting with the UN Conference on the Human Environment in Stockholm in 1972, a simultaneous "NGO forum" became a standard feature of UN activity. The forums allowed people from NGOs in different countries to gather in one place, discuss the issues being addressed, and develop joint statements about them to be presented to the government delegates at the global conference. As democratization spread at the national level in the 1980s, UN human rights bodies and NGOs came into greater contact. When the UN Conference on Environment and Development met in Rio in 1992, NGOs secured a formal place in the institutional follow-up through the Commission on Sustainable Development, and similar arrangements followed other global summits. As the twentieth century ended, then, NGOs were becoming more and more prominent in United Nations activity.

This prominence led to proposals that NGOs should also interact directly with the General Assembly. Yet there were also concerns about the extent to which NGOs in general or any particular NGO were representative of the persons for whom it claimed to speak. The problem was two-fold: doubts that the majority of NGOs, which were based in industrial countries, could speak for persons in developing countries, and questions of whether and how much an NGO's leadership was actually chosen by or accountable to its members. While some NGOs have large memberships and explicit procedures for selecting leaders and periodically reviewing their performance, other NGOs consist of a few people having access to a telephone, a fax machine, a computer, an Internet connection, and website hosting. NGO leaderships were certainly distinct from governments, and understood their interests differently than governments, but many observers saw no reason to believe that they were actually any more representative of ordinary people around the world then national governments.

Whether or not inspired by the example of the European Parliament, which added a directly chosen popular element to the institutions of the European Community (now European Union), several advocates of UN reform began discussing the desirability of establishing some UN organ tied directly to the peoples, rather than to the governments, of member states, in the 1980s.[15] In some versions, a "peoples' assembly" would become a second chamber of the General Assembly. In others, a "parliamentary assembly" distinct from the current intergovernmental assembly would evolve gradually. It would begin as an advisory body with members chosen by national parliaments, and evolve over time into a body with decision-making authority and members elected by popular vote.

The experience of the European Parliament suggests that any peoples' or parliamentary assembly would attract interest and attention to the extent that it had authority over things that matter directly to the peoples. There was little interest in the European Parliament until it acquired a direct role in the budget process and the ability to affect executive decision-making by voting to dismiss the entire Commission. The European Union is today a considerable distance down the road toward supranational integration of its 25 member states. The United Nations, in contrast, remains a league of states organized to facilitate co-operation among the members but not their eventual amalgamation into a single political unit. As long as the United Nations remains a league of states, the politics that really affect the peoples of the world will continue to occur primarily at the national level or regional level. Globalization has significantly changed the context of national or regional politics, making it much harder for any country or group of countries to isolate itself from the rest of the world. The interconnections produced by globalization may trigger a change in the political organization of the international system, and in consequence a change in the nature of the United Nations. Overcoming the "democratic deficit" would be more or less urgent depending on how the international system evolves, a topic to be taken up in Chapter 6.

Notes

1 For instance, Nordic UN Project, The United Nations in Development: Reform Issues in the Economic and Social Fields, Final Report (Stockholm: 1991); Secretary-General (Annan), Renewing the United Nations: A Program for Reform, UN Doc. A/51/950 (14 July 1997); Independent Working Group on the Future of the United Nations, The United Nations in Its Second Half-Century (New York: 1995); Maurice Bertrand, Some Reflections on Reform of the United Nations, UN Doc. JIU/REP/85/9 (Geneva: 1985). This trend continued in studies focused on peacekeeping and conflict resolution. See the Report of the Panel on United Nations Peace Operations, UN Doc. A/55/305-S/2000/809 of 21 August 2000. Accessible at *www.un.org/peace/reports/peace_operations/*.

2 Recounted in Sydney D. Bailey, *The General Assembly of the United Nations* (New York: 1960), 90.

3 Address to the Electors at Bristol, 3 November 1774, in *On Empire, Liberty and Reform: Speeches and Letters of Edmund Burke* (New Haven: Yale University Press, 2000), 55–6.

4 E.g. Remarks at a press conference on April 11, 1961, quoted in André Passeron, ed, *De Gaulle Parle* (Paris, 1962) pp. 405–7.

5 E.g. Pierre Cot, "Winning East–West through North–South," *Foreign Policy* 46: 3–18 (spring 1982).

6 Abe Yeselson and Anthony Gaglione, *A Dangerous Place: The United Nations in World Politics* (New York: 1974); Daniel Patrick Moynihan, *A Dangerous Place* (Boston: 1978); Jeanne Kirkpatrick, *Dictatorships and Double Standards* (New York: 1982).

7 This number understates the increase because four of the numbered items were clusters of two to five subitems in 1946 whereas 21 of the 165 numbered items were clusters of two to 26 subitems in 2003. Compare *General Assembly Official Records, Plenary Meetings, First Session*, part 1, 33–4 and part 2, L–LII (the pagination style changes between the two parts.) with UN Doc. A/58/150 of 18 July 2003.

8 GA Resolutions 44/146 and 44/147 of 15 December 1989 and 45/150 and 45/151 of 18 December 1990.

9 Yeselson and Gaglione, *A Dangerous Place: The United Nations in World Politics*; Moynihan, *A Dangerous Place*.

10 For example Moynihan, *A Dangerous Place*.

11 E.g. Tower of Babble (2004).

12 Populations and medians are drawn from Joseph E. Schwartzberg, *Revitalizing the United Nations* (New York: 2004), 8.

13 Ali A. Mazrui, "The United Nations and some African political attitudes," *International Organization* 18: 513 (1964).

14 E.g. Carol Barrett and Hannah Newcombe, "Weighted voting and international organisations," special issue of *Peace Research Reviews* 2(2) (April 1968); Robert K. Morrow, *Proposals for a More Equitable General Assembly Voting Structure* (Washington: 1989); Schwartzberg, *Revitalizing the United Nations*, 13–14 and 26.

15 E.g. Marc Nerfin, "The future of the United Nations system," *Development Dialogue* 1985: 1; Dieter Heinrich, *The Case for a United Nations Parliamentary Assembly* (Amsterdam: 1992).

6 The General Assembly in the twenty-first century

The turn of any century, but particularly one corresponding to the start of a new millennium, encourages thought about the future. Thus the year 2000 (despite the Western origins of the dating) inspired considerable discussion of what might lie ahead. The United Nations system was no exception, with various bodies holding special sessions to mark the millennium. Most prominent among these were the gatherings sponsored by the General Assembly – the Millennium Summit in August 2000 and the Millennium Assembly that fall. The Millennium Summit brought together national leaders from 149 of the then 189 member states; the Millennium Assembly produced a Millennium Declaration summarizing widely shared visions of what the world should become in the twenty-first century.[1]

The medium-term goals and broad vision of the future expressed in the Millennium Declaration attracted the most public attention, but it also included statements about the future functioning and organization of the United Nations system. The theme of revamping the UN was sounded even more strongly by the Secretary-General's High Level Panel on Threats, Challenges, and Change in December 2004, which proposed two formulas for revising Security Council membership and procedures as well as suggesting a new composition and task for the Economic and Social Council. The High Level Panel also urged the General Assembly to shorten its agenda and focus on the main challenges of the current era, establish smaller and more focused committees, and develop closer engagement with civil society so it could better use its "unique legitimacy in moral terms" to promote desirable goals.[2] Whether any of the High Level Panel's proposals become reality will depend not only on the organizational choices made by member states but also on the shape of the context within which the UN and its members operate. This context, in turn, will depend on how the structure of the international system evolves.

The Millennium Assembly vision

The Millennium Declaration assumes a world of separate states co-operating with each other through the United Nations to establish an international order based on six "fundamental values" – freedom, equality, solidarity, tolerance, respect for nature, and shared responsibility. While these values are to guide governments' domestic and foreign policies, they supplement rather than replace the basic principles of interstate relations established in the Charter. The declaration also records governments' intention to "rededicate ourselves to support all efforts to uphold" six basic norms: 1) respect for the sovereign equality of all states together with their territorial integrity and political independence, 2) resolution of disputes by peaceful means in conformity with the principles of justice and international law, 3) the right to self-determination of peoples still under colonial domination and foreign occupation, 4) non-interference in the internal affairs of states, 5) respect for the equal rights of all without distinction as to race, sex, language, or religion, and 6) mutual co-operation in solving international economic, social, cultural, or humanitarian problems.

Sections II through VII of the Declaration further define these six core values by laying out more specific goals in the areas of international security; economic development, and poverty eradication; environmental protection; human rights, democracy, and good governance; protecting the vulnerable; and meeting the special needs of Africa. Most of these goals are stated in the broad abstract terms familiar in General Assembly resolutions. However, with considerable prodding from Secretary-General Annan to focus particularly on the fates of the poorest people, the goals for poverty reduction are stated in observable quantitative terms. Governments agreed that by 2015 they would:

1   halve the proportion of world population having incomes of less than $1 a day (requiring reduction from the 2000 level of 22 percent to 11 percent);
2   halve the proportion of world population suffering from hunger;
3   halve the proportion of world population unable to reach or afford safe drinking water (requiring reduction from the 2000 level of 20 percent to 10 percent);
4   ensure that all children can complete primary schooling and that females and males have equal access to secondary and higher education;
5   reduce maternal mortality by 75 percent;
6   reduce mortality among children under five by two-thirds;
7   halt and begin to reverse the spread of HIV/AIDS, malaria, and other major human diseases.

An eighth goal, making significant improvements in the lives of at least 100 million slum dwellers, was given a 2020 target date.

Many observers doubt that the world's governments will muster the political will and financial resources needed to meet these goals, and the prospect of success has continued to recede.[3] Even so, this part of the Millennium Declaration marks a breakthrough for the UN system because it is one of the few statements of goals from the General Assembly that specifies verifiable quantitative yardsticks of progress. This has encouraged UN reform discussions to focus on how the UN system's various agencies could be organized to be more effective monitors of national efforts in their various fields.

Section VIII of the Millennium Declaration shifts focus and records governments' views about shaping the United Nations Organization to meet twenty-first-century needs. Combat metaphors dominate the first paragraph, in which governments record their commitment to "spare no effort to make the United Nations a more effective instrument for pursuing all of these priorities: the fight for development for all the peoples of the world; the fight against poverty, ignorance, and disease; the fight against injustice; the fight against violence, terror, and crime; and the fight against the degradation and destruction of our common home." The other paragraphs state commitments to strengthen or reform specific UN organs.

There governments agreed "to reaffirm the central position of the General Assembly as the chief deliberative, policy-making, and representative organ of the United Nations, and to enable it to play that role effectively." The more forward-looking reform ideas are mentioned at the end, in commitments to ensure greater policy coherence and co-operation among UN bodies and agencies, the Bretton Woods institutions, the WTO, and "other multilateral bodies"; strengthen co-operation between the UN and national parliaments; and provide NGOs, civil society, and "the private sector" greater opportunities to contribute to attainment of global goals.

The future international system

As with the substantive goals, whether and to what extent the UN reform suggestions of the Millennium Declaration are adopted depends on choices by many actors at all levels. However, whether the organizational suggestions actually adopted have positive results also depends on the nature of the international system. Political institutions, no less than political actors, operate in the context of a broader social system, and organizational features that work well in one sort of context fail in another. Thus the shape of the UN in the future will be determined not only by the organizational preferences of particular actors, but also on the features of the international system. Thus the roles and functioning of the General Assembly, and indeed of the other parts of the

UN system, depend very much on how that system develops in coming decades.

The future shape of the international system has been the subject of wide speculation since the end of the Cold War. Most of these speculations assume that the international system will continue to display a fair degree of predictability and stability; a minority foresee collapse into confusion.[4] The visions of collapse into confusion foresee little role for the UN, or even most national governments. They anticipate instead formation of smaller units in which those who can organize violence or threats of violence most effectively will intimidate and lord over the rest. The visions of a fairly stable world exist in three main variations, foreseeing a world of states, a world government, or a world of networks. Each variation projects a very different role for the United Nations and in particular for the General Assembly.

The world of states vision assumes that the international system will continue to be decentralized, with most political power held by independent states. Those states will co-operate with one another in varying degrees through a variety of intergovernmental organizations, transgovernmental collaborations, and periodic summits, but will continue to insist on their decision-making autonomy. Though anticipating a strong degree of continuity in the future, even those who foresee a continuing world of states, acknowledge that the increasing interconnection between states and societies developing in a globalized world pose serious challenges for states and require considerable adaptation by governments. However these observers do not accept claims that globalization will inevitably lead to a new world political structure. They do acknowledge that many contemporary states may be merged into a larger territorial entity or fragment into smaller ones, or that a different form of state may arise.[5] Yet they can point to the fact that the state has undergone several transformations in the past to support their belief that some form of territorial state will remain the basic unit of governance in the world.

At least since publication of Immanuel Kant's *Perpetual Peace* in 1797, philosophers and others have projected the vision of a single set of political institutions spanning the entire world. Kant envisioned a league of commercial republics co-operating with each other through a fairly minimal set of central institutions. Others, following the domestic analogy, believe that the problem of attaining global peace and prosperity can be solved only by replicating at the world level the political centralization prevailing within states. Their preferred future involves establishing a world government – a set of governing institutions having authority to make binding rules and capacity to enforce them around the world.

Since 1945 the most persistent proponents of world government have been members of the World Federalist Association, whose institutional vision projects the federal organization of government prevailing in many countries around the world – including Brazil, Canada, Germany, India, the Russian Federation, and the USA – to the global level.[6] In this view, a world federation would replicate on a larger territorial scale the characteristics of federal states: centralized governance of a large area would be combined with safeguards for the local autonomy of one or more layers of distinct subunits. The result, proponents argue, would provide the advantages of both a large economic space and ability to keep politics as close to local communities as possible. The attraction of such visions has been demonstrated by the European Union, which has increasingly emphasized the principle of "subsidiarity" (decisions should be made at the level of the smallest unit capable of handling the problem) as the number of members and the number of issues covered by common policies have increased.

Proponents of world government have suggested two ways of reaching that goal. The first involves agreeing to political union, formally merging states sovereignty and subordinating themselves to the larger unit, then developing the administrative apparatus and sense of social solidarity needed to maintain the union. In federalist versions, political union would entail transferring power over security issues, macroeconomic management, and preservation of democratic institutions to the world level while existing states retain certain powers. The second, the Functionalist vision of David Mitrany or Jean Monnet, would involve a less direct process. States would begin by accepting joint decision-making on certain administrative and technical questions, reap benefits of scale and efficiency from that co-operation, come to perceive that greater benefits would flow if co-operation was extended to additional questions, and end up involved in such extensive co-operation that formal political union merely confirmed what already existed. While the drafters of the UN Charter drew some inspiration from this model, the European Community/ European Union remains the primary exemplar of this process.

A third vision of the future foresees world governance through globe-spanning networks of government agency-based and nongovernmental actors in different parts of the world.[7] These networks might operate through private organizations or associations, such as the International Organization for Standards or the Paris club of major multinational banks. They might equally operate through intergovernmental organizations like the UN Specialized Agencies, the Bank for International Settlements (which links national central banks), or the Group of Seven/Eight summits. They might operate through new or newly reorganized "public/private" institutions or partnerships of which the International Labor Organization or the International Committee of the Red Cross/Red Crescent Societies may be forerunners.

In most visions, governance by network would leave existing territorial boundaries in place, but establish collaborations across boundaries to create larger economic and administrative spaces *de facto* through parallel application of identical rules and standards more able to channel the pressures of globalization. Much of the discussion of the strangely named "neomedievalism"[8] is a variant on this idea, drawing on a core notion that, as in medieval Europe, relations of political super- and subordination would depend on personal linkages rather than geographic proximity defined by administrative boundaries. The likelihood and potential of network-based governance is now a major theme among students of international regimes and international political economy.[9] Today there is also greater awareness that not all networks are benign. There have been highly charged debates among critics of neoliberal versions of globalization about including for-profit private entities (corporations) in governance discussions at the UN and elsewhere. Since September 11 publics, governments, and academics have all become aware that criminals, kleptocrats, hate groups, violent factions, and other undesirables can and do exploit network organizations, leading to a more sophisticated understanding that "network" is a form of organization for collective activity equally available to actors with very divergent goals.

The future General Assembly

Each of these competing visions – a world of states, a world government, and a world of networks – assumes that there will be some coherent pattern of governance at the global level. In the continuing world of states, the United Nations system and the General Assembly would still exist in forms similar to those of today. Attaining world government would require extensive institutional change, either replacing the UN with another set of institutions or thoroughly revamping the UN system to give it the organizational structure, resources, and authority necessary for centralized governance. In a world of networks, the UN system might or might not undergo significant institutional change depending on how the networks organize themselves, co-ordinate with each other, and relate to other actors. Like many in the network discussion, the High Level Panel on Threats, Challenges, and Change assumes that national governments are not going to disappear, though they will exercise a redefined authority in new ways. This led Secretary-General Annan to assert in his foreword to the Panel's Report that "capable and responsible states" will be the main source of action to establish and maintain security, and that the job of the UN is to help states increase their own capacity.[10]

In a world of states, the United Nations system will continue to function as a league of states, an institutional mechanism for co-ordinating the application of state political authority to international problems. Its various organs may be altered in detail, the voting rules might be adjusted, and the numbers and identities of member states might change as existing states merge or dissolve. The administrative and technical activities pursued by Specialized Agencies and other UN bodies would be redefined by changes in technology, knowledge, or beliefs. In a world of states, the General Assembly would continue to be a deliberative body issuing recommendations and specializing in norm-formation. In its more effective moments it would probably operate by consensus rather than by voting for two reasons. First, consensus is held in higher regard than voting in many parts of the world. Second, it would allow individual member states to continue maintaining the consentual theory of international law under which states are legally obliged only when they have clearly consented to an obligation.[11] With political authority still concentrated at the state level, the United Nations budget would remain relatively small and its staff and other resources modest.

Creation of a world government would require thoroughgoing institutional transformation. If that world government took federal form, as seems likely, the United Nations system would have to be transformed into the executive, legislature, judiciary, and administrative organs of the world government. The General Assembly, probably consisting of a chamber of governments (the current plenary) and a chamber of peoples (the oft-proposed elected body), would acquire powers to legislate, tax, and control use of the world government's revenues. Some smaller body – whether an altered Security Council, a global analog to a national cabinet made up of heads of administrative agencies and major Secretariat departments, or something else – would manage the administration and have authority to deal with emergency situations such as massive natural disasters, interstate conflicts about to trigger armed conflict, internal violence beyond the capacity of more localized institutions to handle, and mass human rights violations of the sort that today inspire demands for humanitarian intervention. UN rule-supervisory machinery, like the Commission on Human Rights and the various international courts, would acquire greater power to review national- or regional-level decisions, policies, and actions.

World government would not solve the problem of war, any more than the existence of national governments prevents all armed conflict among individuals and groups within a state. A world government, unlike the current UN, would command sufficient forces of its own to intervene effectively. This would prevent interstate and within-state armed conflicts from spreading very far or lasting very long. It would also minimize the likelihood of others not yet involved joining in. Again like a national government, a world government would be effective in direct measure to its ability to win voluntary consent from the governments and populations of states. This voluntary consent could be elicited by appeals to material interest, prudence, global loyalty (supplementing, not entirely replacing other loyalties), or ethical and moral beliefs. Like national legislatures in the individual states, the global legislature would need to function in such ways that reinforce the plausibility of these appeals. It would need to remind the governments and peoples of states of how they benefit from world government, help instill a sense of prudence and self-restraint, help foster global loyalty, and highlight shared ethical and moral precepts. It would need therefore to exhibit transparency and consistency in applying evenhanded procedures, provide opportunities for reasoned debate, and acknowledge its accountability to the governments and peoples of the world.

The place of the United Nations system in a world of networks is less obvious at first glance. The UN system as a whole, or various parts of it, could become part of the sets of global networks providing effective governance. Yet it or they might also be bypassed as government agencies, business firms, professional organizations, trade unions, interest groups, and social movements form their own transnational policy coalitions. These coalitions might use existing institutions; it is easy to imagine some of them operating through the international financial institutions, the specialized agencies, or multilateral organizations, like the UN Climate Change Secretariat, established to manage particular international regimes. Private actors might also create new institutions of their own, emulating the existing International Organization for Standards, International Association of (Ship) Classification Societies, or World Association of Nuclear Operators.

The new institutions created by particular transnational policy networks would not necessarily pose a threat to the UN system's existence. A division of authority in which they handled some issues while elements of the UN system handled others might well develop. More likely, a combination of UN agencies, intergovernment agency collaborations, and private associations would share the task of regulating various types of activity.[12] The institutions of the UN system would continue to function in their respective areas of competence, from time to time redefining them as needed.

Intergovernmental creations like the Group of Seven, which bring together national leaders and consider a broad agenda rather than any single particular issue, are more likely sources of competition for the General Assembly. The G-7 began as an annual consultation among the leading industrial states on macroeconomic management. Yet as the USA, Western Europe, and Japan faced the question of how to handle the end of the Cold War, it emerged as something like a management council of the great powers. Mikhail Gorbachev perceived the change immediately, and sought an invitation to the 1990 G-7 summit. He was not included, but the Russian Federation was invited to participate in certain G-7 meetings in 1998, inspiring the new nomenclature G-7/G-8. The Group of 77 also perceived the change and asked the G-7 to establish some form of regular meeting with it as well. The G-7 has not been willing to meet with the whole Group of 77, or even with the "Group of 15" formed by several of the G-77's self-declared leaders, but has added sessions with the leaders of developing countries it invites.

The implications of a world of networks for the General Assembly are even less obvious. Such a world could well continue and intensify sidelining the assembly as UN member states took their concerns elsewhere. Though even a world of networks needs deliberative bodies capable of creating, altering, or refining shared norms and understandings, those tasks might be divided among a number of bodies rather than concentrated in any single deliberative forum.

To continue functioning as a global deliberative body in a world of networks, the General Assembly would need to prune out its agenda, focus more effectively on the main issues of the day, and develop some form of direct contact with the nongovernmental actors involved in governance networks. This might involve building on the existing trends towards direct contact between the General Assembly and various sorts of nonstate actor. Yet broadening such contacts would involve the assembly in a new problem, dealing with the cross-pressures created as different NGOs, social movements, or other nonstate actors seek to legitimate or delegitimate each other's presence. Such cross-pressures have been felt already. World Population Conferences have been marked by strong contention between "right to life" and "pro-choice" NGOs. Some environmental groups and social movement organizations are profoundly unhappy about the inclusion of business groups on grounds that since business groups already have a lot of influence at the national level the UN should serve as a counterweight to them.

Each possible future – a world of states, a world government, and a world of networks – creates a distinct context having different implications for the existence, structure, and functions of the General Assembly. Thus while it is safe to project that the General Assembly of 2050 will not be the same as the General Assembly of 2005, it is much harder to specify its actual characteristics in that year. Whatever the shape of the future, it is equally safe to conclude that the assembly will be eclipsed by other forums if its members persist in their current practices. Only if the members, particularly the Third World majority, are willing to become much more selective in choosing topics to address each year and to reserve resolutions for comment on weighty developments will they move the General Assembly in a direction making it a more effective deliberative body. Doing so would secure it a prominent place in either a world of states or a world of networks, and put it in a position from which it could evolve into all or part of a world legislature.

Notes

1 General Assembly Resolution 55/2 of 8 September 2000; *UN Yearbook 2000*, 55.

2 Secretary-General's High Level Panel on Threats, Challenges, and Change, *A More Secure World: Our Shared Responsibility* (New York: 2004), par. 240–3. Accessible on the UN's website at *www.un.org/secureworld/*.

3 Sakako Fukuda-Parr, director and lead author of the UNDP *Human Development Report 2003* concludes that only two of the goals: access to water and reduction in the proportion of persons living under $1 a day will be met by 2015. She also notes that these successes result mainly from significant economic development in China, which is carrying more persons upward than the slow development, economic stagnation, and scattered economic deterioration prevalent in other parts of the world. See her "Millennium development goals: why they matter," *Global Governance* 10(4): 400–1 (2004).

4 Most famously, Robert Kaplan, *The Coming Anarchy: Shattering the Dreams of the Post Cold War* (New York: 2000).

5 Philip Bobbett, *The Shield of Achilles* (Cambridge, MA: 2001) is a particularly fertile source of ideas about different types of state and the ways in which contemporary nation-states might evolve.

6 The current proposals and related studies of the World Federalist Association can be accessed through the website of their Institute for Global Policy, *www.globalpolicy.org/*.

7 James N. Rosenau and Ernst-Otto Czempiel, *Governance without Government* (Cambridge, UK: 1992) was an early expression of network notions. They are now the subject of a large body of academic and more popular writings.

8 The term is drawn from a discussion of potential futures in Hedley Bull, *The Anarchical Society* (London: 1977), 254–5.

9 *Global Governance*, which describes itself as "a journal of multilateralism and international organizations," devotes considerable attention to debate about defining the term "global governance" and to discussions of networks.

10 Secretary-General Kofi Annan, "Foreword" to *A More Secure World: Our Shared Responsibility*, vii.

11 The unusual spelling "consentual" is intended to highlight the emphasis on individual states' consent more clearly than the international lawyers' more common "consensual."

12 John Braithwaite and Peter Drahos, *Global Business Regulation* (Cambridge, UK: 2000) provide many examples.

Select bibliography and electronic resources

Institutional features of the General Assembly

Baehr, Peter R. (1970) *The Role of a National Delegation in the General Assembly*, New York: Carnegie Endowment for International Peace Occasional Paper No. 9.

Bailey, Sydney D. (1964) *The General Assembly of the United Nations*, rev. edn, New York: Praeger.

Cocke, Earle, Jnr (1959) "The United Nations General Assembly – a captive of its own procedures," *Vanderbilt Law Review* 13: 651–62.

Goodrich, Leland M. (1951) "Development of the General Assembly," *International Conciliation* Number 471.

Hovey, Allen, Jnr (1951) "Obstructionism and the rules of the General Assembly," *International Organization* 5: 515–30.

Peterson, M.J. (1986) *The General Assembly in World Politics*, London: George Allen & Unwin.

Queneudec, Jean-Pierre (1965) "Le president de l'Assemblee Generale de l'Organization des Nations Unis," *Revue generale de droit international public* 70: 878–915.

Analyses of the UN Charter

Cot, Jean-Pierre and Pellet, Alain (eds) (1991) *La Chartre des Nations Unies: commentaire article par article*, 2nd edn, Paris: Economia.

Goodrich, Leland M., Hambro, Edvard, and Simons, Anne P. (1967) *Charter of the United Nations: Commentary and Documents*, 3rd edn, New York: Columbia University Press.

Simma, Bruno (ed.) (1991) *Charta der Vereinten Nationen: Kommantar*, Munich: C.H. Beck.

——— (1995) *Charter of the United Nations: A Commentary*, Oxford: Oxford University Press. English-language expanded edition of *Charta der Vereinen Nationen*.

Politics in the General Assembly

Alker, Hayward R. and Russett, Bruce M. (1965) *World Politics in the General Assembly*, New Haven: Yale University Press.

Daws, Sam (2003) "Groups in the United Nations," in Ramesh Thakur (ed.) *What Is Equitable Geographic Representation in the 21st Century?* Tokyo: United Nations University.

Farajallah, Samaan Boutros (1963) *La Groupe Afro-Asiatique dans le Cadre des Nations Unies*, Geneva: Librairie Droz.

Hovet, Thomas, Jnr (1960) *Bloc Politics in the United Nations*, Cambridge, MA: Harvard University Press.

Jacobsen, Kurt (1978) *The General Assembly of the United Nations: A Quantitative Analysis of Conflict, Inequality, and Relevance*, Oslo, Norway: Universitetsforlaget.

Keohane, Robert O. (1967) "The study of political influence in the General Assembly," *International Organization* 21(2): 221–37 (spring).

Kolassa, Jan (1967) *Rules of Procedure of the United Nations General Assembly*, Wroclaw, Poland: Academy of Arts and Sciences of Wroclaw.

Marin-Bosch, Miguel (1994) *Votas y vetos en la Assemblea General de las Nacions Unidas*, Mexico City: Secretaria de Relaciones Exteriores, Fondo de Cultura Economica.

—— (1998) *Votes in the UN General Assembly*, The Hague: Kluwer Law International. Revised and abridged English-language version of *Votas y vetos*.

Riggs, Robert E. (1958) *Politics in the United Nations: A Study of United States Influence in the General Assembly*, Urbana: University of Illinois Press.

Smith, Courtney (2005) *Politics and Process at the United Nations: The Global Dance*, Boulder, CO: Lynne Reinner Publishers.

Recent commentary by participants and close observers

Alger, Chadwick, Lyons, Gene M., and Trent, John E. (eds) (1995) *The United Nations System: The Politics of Member States*, Tokyo: United Nations University Press. Comments on the evolution of various countries' diplomacy at the UN by senior diplomatic or government figures.

Dijkzeul, Dennis and Beigbeder, Yves (eds) (2003) *Rethinking International Organizations: Pathologies and Promise*, New York and Oxford: Berghahn Books. Reflections on various aspects of the UN system by close observers.

Fasulo, Linda (2004) *An Insider's Guide to the UN*, New Haven, CT: Yale University Press. A New York-based journalist's view of the contemporary UN scene.

Jakobson, Max (1993) *The United Nations in the 1990s: A Second Chance?* New York: Twentieth Century Fund. Reflections on the broad course of politics in UN bodies and prospects for the post-Cold War world by an experienced Finnish delegate (Finnish ambassador to the UN 1965- 72.

Mahbubani, Kishore (2003) "The United Nations and the United States: an indispensable partnership," in David Malone and Yuen Foong Khong (eds) *Unilateralism and US Foreign Policy: International Perspectives*, Boulder, CO: Lynne Reinner Publishers, 139–52. The Singaporan ambassador to the UN explains why the General Assembly, even in its most apparently anti-US moments, is actually useful to "the world's only superpower."

Meisler, Stanley (1995) *United Nations: The First Fifty Years*, New York: Atlantic Monthly Press. A *Los Angeles Times* journalist, acknowledging help from EU

Observer Angel Vinas and Venezuelan ambassador Diego Arrida, summarizes the first half-century.

Narasimhan, C.V. (1988) *The United Nations: An Insider's View*, New Delhi: Vikas Publishing House Pvt Ltd. Reflections of an Indian Secretariat member who served as chef de cabinet to Secretaries-General Hammarskjöld, U Thant, and Waldheim.

Smouts, Marie-Claude (1999) "United Nations reform: a strategy of avoidance," in Michael G. Schechter (ed.) *Innovation in Multilateralism*, Tokyo: United Nations University Press, 29–41. A French observer's trenchant comments on the collective ability to talk endlessly.

Taylor, Paul and Groom, A.J.R. (eds) (2000) *The United Nations at the Millennium: The Principal Organs*, London and New York: Continuum. British academics and diplomats look at the UN's main organs.

The evolution of conference diplomacy

Jessup, Philip (1956) "Parliamentary diplomacy," *Recueil des cours* 89: 181–320, Hague Academy of International Law.

Kaufman, Johan (1980) *United Nations Decision Making*, Alphen aan den Rijn: Sijthoff anf Nordhoff.

—— (1988) *Conference Diplomacy: An Introductory Analysis*, 2nd rev. edn, Dordrecht, Netherlands: Martinus Nijhoff for the UN Institute for Training and Research (UNITAR).

Sabel, Robbie (1997) *Procedure at International Conferences: A Study of the Rules of Procedure of Conferences and Assemblies of International Inter-governmental Organizations*, Cambridge, UK: Cambridge University Press.

Summaries of assembly deliberations

A Global Agenda: Issues before the General Assembly, New York: United Nations Association of the USA. Annual roundup produced during the summer detailing likely assembly handling of the issues on its agenda for the upcoming session.

United Nations Handbook, Wellington: New Zealand Ministry of External Relations and Trade. Annual compilation of useful information.

Yearbook of the United Nations, New York: UN Department of Public Information. Annual summary of assembly debates and decisions, typically running four–five years behind current.

Electronic resources

www.un.org

The United Nations' main website, maintained in Arabic, Chinese, English, French, Russian, and Spanish.

www.unaa.org.au

United Nations of Australia. Most material details the organization's own activities, but some portions present Australian positions.

www.unac.org

United Nations Association of Canada. Most material is devoted to the organization's own activities, but some portions present Canadian positions or initiatives at the UN.

www.unanz.org.nz

United Nations Association of New Zealand.

www.ykliitto.fi

United Nations Association of Finland. Primarily Finnish-language material on issues being considered in UN bodies and accounts of organizational activities.

www.fn-sambandet.no

United Nations Association of Norway. Primarily Norwegian-language material on issues considered in UN bodies.

www.sfn.se

United Nations Association of Sweden. Swedish-language material on issues considered in UN bodies.

www.dgvn.de

United Nations Association of Germany. German-language materials on the UN and issues being considered in UN bodies.

www.una-usa.org

United Nations Association of the USA.

Index

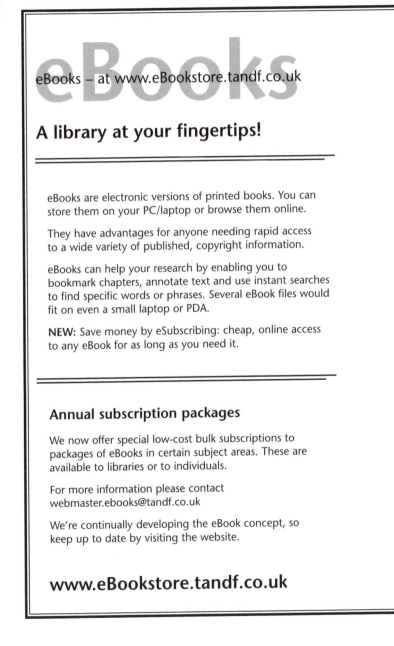